ASSESSMENT AND TREATMENT OF
ADOLESCENT SEX OFFENDERS

Garry P. Perry, MA
Janet Orchard, PhD, CPsych

Professional Resource Press
Sarasota, Florida

PREFACE

This book developed out of our determination to provide a helpful guide to clinicians interested in working with adolescent sex offenders. That determination emerged from the difficulty we experienced in finding resource material to help us understand adolescent sex offenders and provide us with direction in designing our treatment approach.

Initially, we were hesitant to work with adolescent sex offenders. However, we soon realized that an understanding of the functioning of these types of clients helped us develop the skills to perform sex offender-specific therapy and to set realistic standards for ourselves. Once these objectives were achieved, these youths became rewarding clients to work with. We gained significant personal satisfaction from realizing that successful therapy helps the individual to alter deviant patterns of functioning and stop offending. This, in turn, reduces the risk to potential victims.

Our initial contact with adolescent sex offenders was prompted by requests from the legal system for court-ordered psychological assessments. We often recommended sex offender-specific treatment in the reports we sent to the courts, even though adolescent sex offenders have traditionally been treated like other conduct-disorder adolescents and given a variety of generic treatments.

Our sex offender-specific treatment began with individual therapy to offenders, moved on to group work, and then incorporated family therapy. With adolescent sex offenders, group therapy is our preferred intervention, because we focus specifically on offense patterns, behaviors, and thoughts. We term our approach as a psychoeducational, psychotherapy group intervention. Although it encompasses some education and skill training, the central focus is on having the adolescent offenders work through their offense patterns (process model) by achieving greater understanding of the intrapersonal and interpersonal factors that contributed to their offenses.

When we realized that there was a need within our province for more clinicians to work with adolescent offenders, we began presenting papers and conducting workshops on the subject. This book follows our workshop format. First we provide general information on adolescent sex offenders and confront some of the myths about that population. Next we focus on therapist issues. Adolescent sex offenders are a difficult population to work with, and we believe that clinicians should engage in self-examination prior to and during the work. We then discuss assessment issues, highlighting the need for a sex offender-specific interview strategy and providing samples of the clinical interviews we have used. The treatment chapter focuses on our group treatment model but also supplies information on individual and family therapy. The final chapter of the book examines techniques and issues related to enhancing the long-term effects of therapeutic interventions with adolescent offenders.

Our theoretical orientation is best summarized as a cognitive-behavioral approach. We focus on assessing and treating the distorted thought processes, lack of emotional awareness, and destructive behaviors of adolescent sex offenders and their families.

Garry P. Perry
March, 1992

Janet Orchard
March, 1992

TABLE OF CONTENTS

Acknowledgements   *iii*

Preface   *v*

1 Introduction   1

2 General Issues with Adolescent
       Sex Offenders   3

3 Classification of Adolescent
       Sex Offenders   17

4 Therapist Issues in Working with
       Adolescent Sex Offenders   21

5 Assessment Procedures   31

6 Treatment   63

7 Community-Based Treatment   67

8 Enhancing Long-Term Effects
       of Therapy   99

9 Conclusions   107

Appendices   109

Appendix A: Sample Guide
             for Interviewing Offenders   111

Appendix B: Sample Interview Guide
             for Parents of Offenders   115

Appendix C: Risk Checklist for Offenders   119

Appendix D: Risk Factor Constellation   123

References   127

Index   135

ASSESSMENT AND
TREATMENT OF
ADOLESCENT SEX OFFENDERS

 Chapter 1

INTRODUCTION

Society has traditionally envisaged the sex offender as an adult male* living a marginal existence (the dirty old man). Any acknowledged incidents of adolescent sexual offenses have been classified as experimentation. However, as more attention has been paid to the treatment of adult sex offenders, these myths have been shattered. Contrary to the "dirty old man" image, most adult sex offenders are heterosexual men who appear to have normal relationships with adults, including consenting adult sexual relationships (Ross, Loss, & Associates, 1988). Sex offenders come from all age groups: adults (Groth & Birnbaum, 1979); adolescents (Perry & Orchard, 1989); and young children (Johnson & Berry, 1989). Offending behavior by adolescents is not experimentation. Rather, it represents a pattern of deviant behavior that will tend to persist and increase in frequency and severity (Abel, 1984).

Society has recently acknowledged the tremendous danger posed by adolescent sex offenders and has turned to mental-health professionals for a solution (Rogers, 1988). In our efforts to respond, we have realized that traditional therapeutic techniques must be modified to be effective with this population.

---

*For ease of expression, the masculine pronoun is used throughout this book to describe adolescent sex offenders. This does not imply any belief that adolescent females cannot be sex offenders. We have worked with a number of female offenders, and useful literature exists dealing specifically with female sex offenders (e.g., Knopp & Lackey, 1987a).

Unique characteristics of the sex offender require specialized assessment and treatment skills.

The purpose of this book is to provide clinicians with a structured guide to the establishment of an assessment and treatment program for adolescent sex offenders. We will discuss (a) general issues in adolescent sex offending; (b) therapist issues in working with this population; (c) assessment procedures; (d) treatment; (e) community-based treatment; and (f) enhancement of the long-term effects of therapy, followed by our conclusions.

Chapter 2

GENERAL ISSUES WITH
ADOLESCENT SEX OFFENDERS

Our review of the literature, clinical experience, and workshop presentations have taught us that professionals interested in helping adolescent sex offenders must become aware of the characteristics and typology of this population prior to attempting to work with them. As we have interacted with professionals in various disciplines, we have been struck by how often those professionals are influenced by their training and work with nonoffending groups to believe that sex offenders can be treated like voluntary, self-motivated clients. Often, professionals are taken aback by the recognition that sex offenders will attempt to mislead and manipulate the therapist in order to avoid change. To resolve those feelings of discomfort associated with working with an involuntary population, professionals must become familiar with the existing literature concerning the personality styles, thinking patterns, and typical offense patterns of the sex offender. In the ensuing chapters, we will present general information concerning the characteristics of adolescent sex offenders and discuss a typology of adolescent sex offenders. We will highlight and refute commonly held myths about sex offenders with research and clinical evidence.

As recently as the 1970s, societal response to the aggressive sexual behaviors of adolescents frequently involved minimization of the seriousness of those offenses (Groth & Loredo, 1981). That climate of denial was likely the product of many factors, including the (a) shame and fear of the victims, which contributed to underreporting; (b) unwillingness of the sex offenders to receive treatment; (c) deficits in the knowledge bases of various human-service providers; and (d) misdirected desire to protect youthful offenders from stigmatization (Knopp, 1982). That protective stance was expressed at various levels, beginning with treatment workers who declared the offenses to be simply adolescent experimentation and police officers who interpreted the behavior as an isolated event that would not be repeated, and culminating in the court system with plea-bargaining to lesser charges (Bengis, 1986; Knopp, 1982).

More recently, however, adolescent sexual offending has been seen to require specialized assessment and treatment. Four groups of research findings have highlighted the importance of responding to the needs of those youths. First, studies of adult sexual offenders have indicated that initial offenses tend to occur at very early ages, even as early as age 8 or 9 (Groth, Longo, & McFaden, 1982; Johnson & Berry, 1989). One review found that 50% of all adult sex offenders began offending in adolescence (Abel, 1984). A second group of research has revealed evidence to indicate that the severity of offending behavior may escalate when there is no treatment. Longo and Groth (1983) reported that, of the incarcerated adult sex offenders they interviewed, 35% reported progression from compulsive masturbation, exhibitionism, and voyeurism as youths to the more serious sexually aggressive behaviors for which they had been convicted as adults.

Research also indicates that the adolescent sex offender poses an alarming risk to the community (Toufexis, 1989). Abel (1984) observed that the average adolescent male sex offender can be expected to create 380 victims during his lifetime, a 55-fold increase in the number of victims from adolescence to adulthood.

Finally, interventions during adolescence may be more successful because deviant arousal patterns may be less entrenched than in adult offenders (Abel, 1984; Bengis, 1986; Perry & Orchard, 1989). Lanyon (1986), in his review of the literature, suggested that clinicians and researchers need to focus on working with adolescent offenders. He stated that from the viewpoint of early intervention, primary attention should be given to adolescent offenders.

DEFINITIONS

To design an assessment and treatment program for adolescent sex offenders, it is necessary to develop a clear definition of the population to be served. Fortunately for the clinician and the researcher, there exist consistent definitions of the adolescent sex offender, differing only in the upper age limits of adolescence.

DEFINITION OF AN ADOLESCENT SEX OFFENDER

We define the adolescent sex offender as a youth (male or female) between the ages of 12 and 18 years who engages in sexual behavior deemed by society to be inappropriate (e.g., rape, exhibitionism). Sexual offenses include both coercive or nonconsensual sexual acts, including oral and vaginal penetration (by penis, hand, or other objects) or sexual touching and fondling, and so-called hands-off offenses such as exhibitionism, voyeurism, and obscene telephone calls. By law, children are considered too young to give consent. Therefore, any sexual interaction between an adolescent and a younger child is regarded as an offense whether or not force is used (Davis & Leitenberg, 1987).

Professionals should keep in mind that sexual assault is not primarily a sexually motivated behavior. It is usually an offense of aggression or control toward others that is expressed sexually. Sexual assault is an abuse of power which is often unrelated to sexual stimulation or satisfaction. Our experience indicates that most adolescent sexual offenses are planned, rather than the result of impulsive acts.

An analogy may be drawn between alcoholics and sexual offenders. Alcoholics do not drink simply out of thirst, but for a wide range of psychological reasons including low self-esteem, depression, feelings of failure in their career or at home, anger, and so on. Similarly, to say that sex offenders commit sexual offenses because they are desperate for sex or affection, or are overwhelmed by uncontrollable sexual desire, is to overly simplify a complex problem. Sex offenders use assaultive, exploitive sex to meet numerous basic emotional, personal, and social needs. As Richardson, Loss, and Ross (1988) write, "They are using sex to meet these non-sexual needs in a destructive manner" (p. 11). They believe sexual offenses are committed for a number of reasons: (a) to overpower someone, be in control; (b) to achieve revenge against someone or the world; (c) to release anger; (d) to scare someone and make him or her feel bad about himself or herself; (e) immediate gratification (satisfaction of immediate needs); (f) to feel wanted; and (g) to impress someone and feel like someone looks up to you.

DEFINITION OF ADOLESCENT SEX OFFENDER-SPECIFIC TREATMENT

We define sex offender-specific treatment as being composed of therapeutic interventions that focus specifically on the adolescent offender's sexual offenses. Therapy must address the offender's thinking errors, deviant arousal patterns and values, and deviant behaviors. Bengis (1986), Breer (1987), and Perry and Orchard (1989) have all hypothesized that the adolescent's sexual offending must be treated first. Once he begins to understand his deviant arousal patterns and behaviors, interventions can be introduced to treat various other problems.

The first step in sex offender-specific treatment is the completion of a detailed adolescent sex offender-specific assessment. This assessment focuses on assessing the offender's deviant arousal patterns, cognitive distortions, and inappropriate sexual behaviors. The examiner must assess the offender's risk of reoffending and make recommendations about his treatment and placement.

These treatment and placement options will vary for each offender. Some offenders will need closed-custody placements while others can be placed in the community. Some offenders are appropriate for community-based treatment programs while others will need residential treatment; still others might not be appropriate for any treatment program. Decisions regarding treatment and placement must give primary emphasis to the protection of the community.

In the past, clinicians have assumed that generic treatment services or skill-training programs were sufficient interventions to alter offenders' deviant arousal patterns and behaviors. Our clinical experience and that of many others (Bengis, 1986; Bengis & Cunninggim, 1989; Bera, 1989; Coleman, 1988; Ross et al., 1988) has indicated that these types of interventions have not been sufficient to transform the offender. They can be used in conjunction with sex offender treatment but should not be offered as the only interventions for sex offending.

MYTHS

Therapists interested in working with adolescent sex offenders need to become aware of some of the commonly held myths concerning this population. These beliefs have contributed to underreporting of offenses and to lack of resource development.

We encourage the reader to examine the extent to which he or she may subscribe to any of the following misconceptions.

1. *Myth:* Most adolescent sexual offending behaviors are only attempts to learn about sex.
   Fact: Adolescent sexual experimentation differs from sexual offending because the former involves consensual peer sexual exploration. Sexually offending behaviors are not experimentation because they are not consensual acts, are not motivated exclusively by sexual desires, and often involve contacts with children who are significantly younger than the offender (by 3 to 5 years).
2. *Myth:* All sex offenders are male.
   Fact: Sex offenders can be either male or female. Society has traditionally reinforced the belief that only males can initiate a sexual assault, and this has led to under-identification of assaults by females (F. Mathews, 1989).
3. *Myth:* White, middle-class adolescents of average or above-average intellectual abilities do not commit sexual offenses.
   Fact: Adolescent sex offenders come from all races, socioeconomic classes, and levels of intellect.
4. *Myth:* The offender does not know his victims.
   Fact: Offenders are frequently known to their victims as trusted people, such as family members, neighbors, or babysitters.
5. *Myth:* The sexually offending behavior will go away with maturity.
   Fact: The evidence from adult offenders contradicts this belief: 50% of adult offenders began offending in adolescence, and, in some cases, the severity of offending patterns escalated with maturity (Abel, 1984; Groth et al., 1982). Adolescent sex offenders are extremely poor predictors of their future sexual behaviors, and are poor managers in that sphere of their lives. Clinicians need to view the adolescent's sexually deviant behavior as a highly habitual sexual preference. They also need to realize that the offender, without treatment, is perpetually vulnerable to his deviant sexual preferences. He will fall prey to re-offense if he does not respect this vulnerability or if he ceases to manage his life in the ways necessary to prevent re-offense. Such a vulnerability model emphasizes that there is no cure, but rather a relative

mastery of serious behavioral problems. It also focuses on the problems inherent in long-term maintenance, and the risk of later relapse.

6. *Myth:* If an adolescent is apprehended and labeled as a sex offender, the label itself may predispose the youth to re-offend.

   Fact: The assumption that the sex offender label will cause lifelong damage to the individual is seen as being of greater significance than the risk of his re-offending. In reality, the average adolescent sex offender can be expected to create 380 victims over a lifetime (Abel, 1984). Unless the offender is identified, he will not receive appropriate treatment and will continue to re-offend. In the face of this frightening risk to the community, the potential deleterious effect of labeling an adolescent as a sex offender becomes less disturbing.

7. *Myth:* Sexual offenses are exclusively motivated by sexual needs.

   Fact: Sexual assaults are not primarily sexually motivated behaviors. They are usually offenses of control or aggression toward others that are expressed sexually.

8. *Myth:* Sexual offenses are a result of sudden, uncontrollable urges.

   Fact: Sexual offenses are planned actions. Offenders purposely select victims and circumstances in which to offend. The adolescent sex offender, in most instances, does not lash out blindly but behaves in a rational way, given his deviant norms. Offenders need to trace their history of re-offending in order to understand the patterns of their offenses.

9. *Myth:* Victimization by an adolescent is not as traumatic as victimization by an adult.

   Fact: Any sexual offense is traumatic because it represents a violation of the victim's emotional and physical space.

10. *Myth:* The first sexual crime for which the adolescent offender is apprehended is generally his first offense.

    Fact: Adolescent offenders usually have committed a number of offenses against either the same victim or a number of victims. The earlier offenses may have gone undetected or may have been mislabeled as experimentation. The assessor can be almost certain that the adolescent sex offender has not sought treatment after his first offense. He has likely diverted his energies to avoiding detection. Ross et al. (1988) have reported that the average age of child abuse-oriented offenders (offenders who sexually assault children) at the time of their first offense is 15 years old, and the average age at which they receive treatment is 33 years old. For peer age sexual assault-oriented offenders (offenders who assault same-age peers or older people), the average age at the time of the first assault is 18 years old, and the average age for first receiving treatment is 40 years old. Both groups of offenders show this gap between onset of offending and receipt of treatment.

11. *Myth:* Sexual offending can be treated by addressing other problems.
    Fact: Adolescent sex offenders require sex offender-specific treatment to address the thinking errors, deviant arousal patterns, and values that maintain offending behaviors. Generic therapy or social-skills training do not specifically address these problems. Adolescent sex offenders can benefit from various adjunctive therapies (e.g., assertiveness training), but only if offered in conjunction with sex offender-specific treatment.

12. *Myth:* All adolescent sex offenders have been victims of sexual abuse.
    Fact: The Davis and Leitenberg (1987) review of the literature indicated that the factors that predispose an adolescent to commit sexual offenses have yet to be established. Clinical findings must continue to be pursued in research. Thus far the major predeterminant that the majority of adolescent sex offenders have been demonstrated to share is a history of physical abuse. Contrary to the assumption that the major cause of sex offending is a history of sexual victimization, Davis and Leitenberg (1987) did not observe a statistically significant prevalence of victimization in the histories of adolescent offenders. Bera (1989) refers to the belief that all offenders must be victims of sexual abuse as the "vampire syndrome," and argues that this assumption insults the large number of adult victims who have never offended. Certainly one should assess for a history of sexual abuse, but one should not jump to the conclusion that, even if present, such victimization is the singular cause of sexual offending. Sexual deviance and sexual offending are

extremely complex behaviors. There are always multiple causes for this problem. It is erroneous to postulate a single cause, whether it be victimization, family dysfunction, exploratory behaviors, or others.

Numerous intraindividual and familial factors have been suggested as having etiological significance in the development of adolescent sexual offenders. For example, offenders have been described as having minimal social skills; very low self-esteem; limited ability to effectively express anger; feelings of powerlessness; very distorted, highly stereotyped notions of sexuality and intimate relationships; and childhood exposure to aggression and dominance in the forms of sexual, physical, or emotional abuse (Davis & Leitenberg, 1987; Jackson, 1984).

The research investigating these factors suffers from major methodological problems. Only one factor has been confirmed: adolescent sex offenders more often have a history of physical (and likely sexual) abuse than do other groups of male adolescents (Lewis, Shanok, & Pincus, 1981; Van Ness, 1984). Nevertheless, clinical experience should continue to be the impetus for scientific investigations examining the roles of the previous factors in contributing to patterns of sexually offending behavior.

FOCI FOR THERAPY

Most of the adolescent sex offenders with whom we have worked have presented numerous intrapersonal and interpersonal difficulties. Although these problems cannot be assumed to cause the sex offending, they still must be addressed in therapy because they interfere with the youth's ability to achieve a satisfactory adjustment. Table 1 (p. 11) provides an overview of some of the problem areas that should be addressed as components of a total intervention strategy. It is often difficult for clinicians to determine in which problem area to begin interventions. Our experience, and that of others (e.g., Bengis, 1986; Breer, 1987), has indicated that the adolescent's sexually offending behaviors and thoughts need to be treated first. Once the adolescent begins to understand his deviant behavior and arousal patterns, interventions can be introduced to treat various other problems (e.g., lack of social skills, family problems).

As in work with other populations, therapists working with adolescent sex offenders need to become familiar with the factors that have affected the adolescent sex offender's development. Table 1 provides a general overview of these factors but does not arrange them in any systematic manner. We have organized the general factors outlined in Table 1 around the following variables: social relationships, affect, cognitions, behaviors, significant others, maturation, and environment. The adolescent sex offender is apt to evidence difficulty in all facets of life.

TABLE 1: INTERPERSONAL AND INTRAPERSONAL PROBLEM AREAS GENERALLY CHARACTERISTIC OF ADOLESCENT SEX OFFENDERS

- Emotionally immature
- Low self-esteem, feels very inadequate about self
- Suppresses most emotions, especially anger
- Lack of communication with parents
- Identifies with younger aged children
- Avoids positive interactions with opposite-sex peers
- Marked concern regarding sexual identity
- Manipulative personal style
- Marginal social development; limited social activities outside the home
- Mother unaffectionate, demanding, intrusive, and belittling
- Father emotionally distant, indifferent, and uninvolved with family
- History of loneliness, school problems, antisocial or nonsocial behavior used to attract attention
- There is usually a progression of offenses (e.g., peeping, exposing, soliciting)
- Sexual offenses are frequently preceded by a warning, such as masturbatory fantasies that predict the occurrence of the outlet
- Selects victims younger than himself
- Sexually deviant behavior is often the offender's defense against anxiety
- To protect self, uses a variety of different mechanisms: denial, rationalization, and projection
- Sex offenses are motivated by a need for recognition, approval, and power

The qualities listed in this table reflect our own observations as well as those of various experts in the area (Bengis, 1986; Breer, 1987; Coleman, 1988; Jackson, 1984; Knopp, 1985).

11

SOCIAL RELATIONSHIPS

Adolescent sex offenders tend to be isolated, feel powerless and inadequate, have an exaggerated need to feel in control, and be socially inadequate and distrustful. The offender may have difficulty making friends, may spend the majority of his leisure time alone, may be reluctant to establish intimate relationships for fear of being controlled or taken advantage of, or may tend to identify and associate with much younger children.

AFFECT

The adolescent sex offender tends to have difficulty identifying, labeling, and communicating his feelings, usually cannot identify feelings in others, and has difficulty being empathic toward others. This inability to discern his own emotional needs and to be sensitive to the feelings of others allows him to continue to offend because he does not understand the emotional reasons for his offending behaviors and he is not stopped by concern for the impact upon his victim. One of the goals of therapy is to help the offender develop empathy for his victims. The first step in this process usually involves teaching the offender how to identify and communicate his own feelings.

COGNITIONS

Offenders tend to (a) use a variety of defense mechanisms (e.g., denial, rationalization, projection) to cope with their commission of aggressive or deviant acts; (b) endorse the rape myth; (c) hold stereotyped perceptions of male and female roles and personalities; (d) fantasize about sexual offenses; and (e) maintain low opinions of themselves. All these cognitive distortions should be confronted in therapy. Adolescent sex offenders' cognitive distortions take the form of beliefs such as "I didn't really hurt her; she must have wanted it because she didn't fight back," or "The victim seduced me," or "The victim wasn't really hurt by the assault because she (or he) still talks to me."

Denial is a central defense mechanism that the adolescent sex offender uses to avoid taking responsibility for his sexual offenses. Salter (1988) has categorized the denial patterns used by adolescent sex offenders into five modes of functioning:

1. Denial of behavior (physical denial, physical denial with family support, psychological denial)
2. Minimization of the extent of behavior
3. Denial of the seriousness of the behavior
4. Denial of responsibility
5. Full admission with responsibility and guilt

These denial patterns are summarized in Table 2 (pp. 14-15).

BEHAVIORS

Part of the assessment process is to delineate the offender's behavioral deficits. The offender usually has poor social skills (e.g., assertiveness, dating, and communication skills) and has difficulty in establishing peer-age relationships due to a lack of skill in initiating and maintaining friendships. Further, the offender often displays inadequate anger management skills, deficits in stress-coping strategies, and a possible history of substance abuse.

SIGNIFICANT OTHERS

The central people in the adolescent sex offender's life can be his parents, siblings, relatives, or other adults. He may come from a broken home or reside in a home with very controlling parents. The offender may have experienced neglect or emotional, physical, or sexual abuse from people responsible for him. His parents may have modeled inappropriate values and distorted perceptions (e.g., attitudes toward women), styles of coping, or thinking patterns that avoid assuming responsibility (e.g., inappropriate use of defense mechanisms).

Because of these factors, the families of offenders should become involved in the assessment and treatment process. This will not always be productive or even possible. For example, in a case where a parent physically or sexually abuses the offender and then avoids taking responsibility for these actions by blaming the offender, he is unlikely to assume responsibility for his offenses, and the family's support for treatment is apt to be absent or dishonest.

TABLE 2: ADOLESCENT SEX-OFFENDER DENIAL PATTERNS OUTLINED BY SALTER (1988)

DENIAL OF BEHAVIOR

Physical Denial. These offenders deny committing a specific offense on a given day at a particular time. They will often be outraged at being accused and persist with protests of their innocence even in the face of clear evidence of guilt. Offenders using this defensive pattern are very resistant to treatment.

Physical Denial with Family Support. Family members support the offender's physical denial. These offenders are the most difficult to work with in treatment because the family is bolstering the denial pattern.

Psychological Denial. Many offenders completely deny the sexual abuse with which they are charged by stating that they would never do such a thing. According to Salter (1988), family denial of a similar nature is less pathological than family denial focused on the specifics of the particular charge and which involves false alibis. This type of denial by family members often simply indicates that the family genuinely believes the young person to be innocent. Once convinced of his guilt, these families are apt to be supportive of treatment.

MINIMIZATION OF THE EXTENT OF THE BEHAVIOR

Often offenders will admit part but not all of the offenses; for example, they may admit to oral sex but deny intercourse. Such offenders refuse to acknowledge either sexual fantasies or planning offenses. They also typically minimize the extent of harm caused to their victims. They may appear superficially to be remorseful while having no real sense of guilt. They are apt not to acknowledge the difficulty of change and believe that because they have decided not to re-offend, they won't.

DENIAL OF THE SERIOUSNESS OF THE BEHAVIOR

Even upon having admitted to all of the offenses, offenders minimize the seriousness of the consequences of their behavior. They believe that the offenses were not so horrible and are not truly empathic with their victims. Denial of seriousness allows offenders to avoid facing the guilt brought about by recognizing the long-term negative impact of their behavior. These people are at risk of re-offending because believing their behavior wasn't harmful means it is okay to do it again.

Such offenders are apt to argue that they do not need treatment because change will be easy. Indeed, they may assert that therapy will be detrimental because it will make them dwell on the sexual offenses. Change by "not thinking" means that the offender will not have learned coping strategies.

DENIAL OF RESPONSIBILITY

These offenders admit to the behavior and acknowledge that it was wrong but still shirk responsibility. This may be overt, as in those who blame alcohol, or more subtle, as in those who blame the worries of their lives on neglectful behavior by others or the provocative actions of the victim. They do not admit to having gained pleasure from the offenses, nor to have fantasized about them or planned them.

FULL ADMISSION WITH RESPONSIBILITY AND GUILT

These offenders admit the entirety of their offending behavior. Their description matches that of the victim. They are able to describe the antecedents of the offenses, including thoughts or fantasies, and planning of the offenses. They are conscious of the need to strategize to avoid re-offending. They are aware of the lasting harm they have done and are apt to feel depressed.

MATURATION

Like all adolescents, the offender is affected by the physical and emotional maturation process (e.g., changes in physical appearance, emerging genital sexuality, and a desire to separate from family). However, these factors create additional stress for the offender due to other difficulties and inadequacies he is facing. The offender lacks the cognitive development, behavioral skills, life experiences, and family support to learn and grow from these naturally occurring changes.

ENVIRONMENT

In order for him to commit an offense, the adolescent sex offender's environment must provide him with access to victims either directly (through the presence of younger siblings) or indirectly (through proximity to other chosen victims; for example, by babysitting). One of the central concerns in planning interventions with offenders is to place them in an environment that does not allow them access to victims, but that does allow them access to treatment. For those who have abused siblings, this will mean temporary removal from the home. For those who have committed offenses against individuals outside the family, this will mean either family monitoring to eliminate access to victims or, if such monitoring is unreliable, removal from the home. Other sources of environmental influence include the school, social groups (e.g., church clubs), and peer groups. Some offenders do not attend school, do not belong to any social groups, and have no friends. They spend the majority of their time at home which allows them time to fantasize about their assaults. Other offenders associate with a delinquent peer group that confirms their deviant, exploitive values.

Chapter 3

CLASSIFICATION OF
ADOLESCENT SEX OFFENDERS

The therapist working with an adolescent sex offender should carefully explore all the factors that have interacted to lead the adolescent into becoming a sex offender. Once the data have been collected, the therapist can turn to a system of classifying the offender. A number of systems have been developed to classify adult offenders (e.g., Araji & Finkelhor, 1985; Groth, 1982), but they have been of limited use with adolescent offenders. Consequently, several therapists working with adolescent offenders have attempted to develop descriptive typologies specific to that group (e.g., Bera, 1985, 1989; O'Brien & Bera, 1986; Ross et al., 1988). We have found the typology designed by Bera (1985, 1989) and O'Brien and Bera (1986) to be a useful method of conceptualizing adolescent sex offenders. Their system contains seven levels for classifying adolescent sex offenders:

Type 1: Naïve Experimenter. This type tends to be young (11 to 14 years), with little history of acting-out behavior. He is sexually naïve and engages in one or only a few sexually exploratory acts with a younger child (2 to 6 years), using no force or threats.

Type 2: Undersocialized Child Exploiter. The undersocialized child exploiter evidences chronic social isolation and social incompetence. His abusive behavior is likely to be chronic and includes manipulation, rewards, or other enticement. He is

17

motivated to offend by a desire for greater self-importance and for intimacy.

Type 3: Pseudo-Socialized Child Exploiter. The pseudo-socialized exploiter has good social skills and little acting-out history, and is apt to present as self-confident. He may be a victim of some form of abuse. His abuse is likely to have been going on for years. He tends to be motivated by a desire for sexual pleasure through exploitation, tends to rationalize assaults, and feels little guilt or remorse.

Type 4: Sexual Aggressive. The sexual aggressive comes from an abusive, chaotic family. He is more likely to have a long history of antisocial acts, poor impulse control, and substance abuse. His sexual assaults involve force. He is motivated to offend by a desire to experience power by domination, to express anger, and to humiliate his victim.

Type 5: Sexual Compulsive. The sexual compulsive's family is usually emotionally repressive and rigidly enmeshed. His offenses are repetitive, often of a compulsive nature, and are more likely to be hands-off (e.g., peeping or exposing). His motivation for offending may be the alleviation of anxiety.

Type 6: Disturbed Impulsive. The disturbed impulsive is likely to have a history of psychological disorder, severe family dysfunction, substance abuse, and significant learning problems. His offenses are impulsive and reflect disturbance of reality testing.

Type 7: Group-Influenced. The group-influenced offender is apt to be a younger teen with no previous delinquent history who engages in assault in the company of a peer group. The motivation is apt to be peer pressure and the desire for approval.

This typology system is very helpful in planning treatment and residence placements for adolescent sex offenders. Bera (1985, 1989) and O'Brien and Bera (1986) have formulated treatment approaches specific to each type of offender.

Nontrained individuals either (a) tend to lump adolescent sex offenders under one category and treat them all using the same program; or (b) try to define the adolescent sex offender using an adult classification system. Adolescent sex offenders need to be considered as a separate population of sex offenders, and the various types will need different treatment programs and access to various placement options. We have termed this delivery of services a "continuum-of-service model" (Orchard & Perry, 1989).

Chapter 4

THERAPIST ISSUES IN WORKING WITH ADOLESCENT SEX OFFENDERS

The topics of sexuality and sexual aggression are emotionally laden and difficult to discuss. Therapists who consider working with adolescent sex offenders need to increase their awareness of their own sexual attitudes and beliefs, because those values will influence how they relate to and work with adolescent sex offenders. There are two ways in which therapist values may influence therapy:

1. A major impediment to the therapeutic process with adolescent sex offenders is a therapist's communication of rigid, stereotyped attitudes toward sexuality; for example, adherence to rape myths.
2. Therapists need to monitor their emotional responses to discussions about sexual aggression and to elements of the therapeutic process. For example, we have found that clinicians who are not experienced in working with adolescent sex offenders frequently respond with revulsion to discussion of specific offenses or to treatment activities (e.g., masturbatory reconditioning).

In addition to awareness of their perceptions and attitudes toward sexuality and adolescent sex offenders, clinicians interested in working with adolescent sex offenders need special training. The National Task Force Report on Juvenile Sexual Offending (1988) outlined the personal and professional qualities a clinician should possess in order to competently provide offense-specific

21

services to adolescent sex offenders. We have restructured, expanded, and added to the points outlined by the Task Force. The four areas of concern are personal issues, general clinical skills, prerequisite professional qualities, and offender-specific professional qualifications.

PERSONAL ISSUES

Bengis (1988) has outlined some personal concerns important to therapists who work with adolescent sex offenders:

1. Clinicians need to be aware of their perception of healthy sexuality and how they define consensual sex. They must feel comfortable discussing sex. The content of the work will highlight the clinician's sexual values, and those personal beliefs should not take the clinician by surprise.
2. Events discussed by sexual offenders and processing these events with the co-leader may lead to sexual arousal, including sexual feelings toward the co-leader. These feelings should be discussed with the co-leader.
3. Clinicians who have been sexually abused and who work with adolescent sex offenders need to be aware that details from certain cases may arouse intense feelings in themselves associated with their own abuse. They need to discuss these issues with their co-workers; attempts to suppress these issues will only intensify problems.
4. Even for those with no personal history of abuse, the deviant sexuality described by offenders may arouse feelings of sadness, horror, or hopelessness in the therapist. Those reactions must be acknowledged and shared with a co-leader.

COPING WITH PERSONAL REACTIONS

Our experience in training clinicians to work with adolescent sex offenders has revealed that some clinicians believe they can turn off their own thoughts and emotions concerning sexuality and work with offenders in a very objective manner. This style of coping is not useful when working with adolescent sex offenders. There are many approaches to this issue that will encourage clinicians to think about their own values and their perceptions of adolescent offenders. Some represent modifications of Bengis'

(1988) approach, and others originate with us. Two examples are included here.

Example 1. Clinicians should first identify some of the personal issues they might experience in working with adolescent sex offenders, using these and other statements as prompts:

1. My definition of healthy sexuality is _____.
2. My biggest concern or fear about engaging in sex offender work is _____.
3. If I had to listen to a sex offender describe his or her offenses in detail, I would feel _____.
4. If I had to talk with a male offender about his sexual activities with another male, I would feel _____.
5. If I had to listen to an offender talk about sex with a child, I would feel _____.
6. What areas about my own sexuality do I need to deal with if I plan to work with adolescent sex offenders (please list areas)? _____.

Writing out one's responses to these statements forces an assessment of one's own issues. Clinicians may wish to ask coworkers to respond also, and discuss the results.

Example 2. A value-clarification exercise called "The Alligator River Exercise" helps clinicians explore their perceptions about sexual abuse. This technique is also useful in working with offenders. Instructions are to read the following narrative, rate the five characters in the story from most despicable (1) to least despicable (5), and write out the reasons for your ratings.

Once upon a time there was a woman named Abigail who was in love with a man named Gregory. Gregory lived on the shore of a river. Abigail lived on the opposite shore of the river. The river which separated the two lovers was teeming with man-eating alligators. Abigail wanted to cross the river to be with Gregory. Unfortunately, the bridge had been washed out. So she went to ask Sinbad, a riverboat captain, to take her across. He said he would be glad to if she would consent to go to bed with him preceding the voyage. She promptly refused and went to a friend named Ivan to explain her plight. Ivan did not want to be involved at all in the situation. Abigail felt her only alternative was to accept Sinbad's terms. Sinbad fulfilled his promise to Abigail and delivered her into the arms of Gregory. When she told Gregory about her amorous escapade in order to cross the river, Gregory cast her aside with disdain. Heartsick and dejected, Abigail turned to Slug with her tale of woe. Slug, feeling compassion for Abigail, sought out Gregory and beat him brutally. Abigail was overjoyed at the sight of Gregory getting his due. As the sun sets on the horizon, we hear Abigail laughing at Gregory. (Simon, Howe, & Kirschenbaum, 1978, pp. 291-292)

Again, it would be helpful to have co-workers complete the exercise and discuss the results. This exercise is useful because it provides information on the clinician's (or offender's) perceptions of victims, sexual assault, responsibility, empathy, cooperation, and consensual versus coercive sex. It is important to discuss how the values involved relate to sexual offenses. Our ratings are as follows:

1. Slug took advantage of Gregory's rejection of Abigail to ingratiate himself to her, and he used violence to respond to feelings.
2. Sinbad sexually assaulted Abigail by abusing power to force her to have sex with him.
3. Gregory's rigid perceptions of purity and loyalty led him to reject Abigail. He was not prepared to empathize with her plight and to see the reasons for her choices. He blamed her for the situation.
4. Ivan chose to be uninvolved, and is therefore like the bystander who knows something is happening and does nothing to help the victim.
5. Abigail is a victim who feels helpless and controlled, first by Sinbad, then by Gregory. Her laughter when Gregory is beaten can be likened to the impotent rage of the victim of sexual abuse.

GENERAL CLINICAL SKILLS

Clinicians interested in working with adolescent sex offenders must possess a number of general clinical skills prior to being trained to work with offenders. These general clinical skills have been identified by the National Task Force (1988) and expanded upon by us.

LISTENING SKILLS

Clinicians must possess the ability to interpret and respond to both verbal and nonverbal messages from the offender. Part of the treatment process will also involve teaching listening skills to the offender.

EMPATHY FOR THE IMPACT OF VICTIMIZATION

The clinician must be able to help the offender develop the knowledge and skills to feel empathy for his victims. If the offender has been a victim of sexual or physical abuse, the therapist must learn how to express empathy to the offender while still holding him responsible for the offenses.

CONFRONTIVE AND SUPPORTIVE SKILLS

Skills in confrontation include the ability to challenge the discrepancies, distortions, smoke screens, and game playing the offender uses, both knowingly and unknowingly. The clinician also needs to be able to challenge the offender to move beyond discussion to action (Egan, 1990). While being confrontive, the clinician must be able to maintain a supportive working relationship. One way of being supportive is to validate the offender for things he does well in his life (e.g., sports).

ABILITY TO SET LIMITS AND HOLD CLIENTS ACCOUNTABLE

Clinical work with adolescent sex offenders does not involve only setting limits in therapy; it also involves setting strict limits for living in the community (e.g., no babysitting) and monitoring the offender. Clinicians must also be able to hold the offender accountable for violations of these limits.

Excellent resource material for helping clinicians develop listening skills, empathy, confrontive and supportive skills, and abilities to set limits and hold clients accountable are W. H. Cormier and L. S. Cormier (1985); Egan (1990); and Evans et al. (1984).

PREREQUISITE
PROFESSIONAL QUALITIES

KNOWLEDGE BASE
IN JUVENILE DELINQUENCY

Clinicians interested in working with adolescent sex offenders must have a thorough understanding of how this population differs from other delinquents. To accomplish this task, they need to understand delinquent development and behaviors (J. D. Burchard & S. N. Burchard, 1987; Finckenauer, 1984; Quay, 1987).

ASSESSMENT SKILLS

Clinicians should have general assessment skills prior to receiving sex offender-specific training. Prerequisite skills include how to structure assessment sessions, collect data, draw conclusions from data, and incorporate data and conclusions in a report. Training in conducting forensic psychological assessments would be a valuable asset (Byrne, 1985; Enfield, 1987; Maloney, 1985; Stout, 1987). We will discuss adolescent sex offender assessments in Chapter 5 of this book.

COURT EXPERIENCE

The clinician should have some training in interacting with the legal system, writing reports, working with probation officers, testifying as an expert witness, and so forth (Anchor, 1984; Blau, 1984; Monahan, 1980; Westphal & Kohn, 1984).

GROUP SKILLS

The primary intervention in treating adolescent sex offenders is a group therapy model that focuses on both education and process. Clinicians who lack training in group psychotherapy will have difficulty conducting adolescent offender groups. After developing generic group skills (e.g., Corder, 1987; Freeman, 1983; Naar, 1982; Rosenbaum, 1983), adolescent sex offender training can help clinicians modify and adapt their knowledge and skills to work with offenders.

OFFENDER-SPECIFIC
PROFESSIONAL QUALIFICATIONS

CONTINUATION OF EDUCATION,
TRAINING, AND EXPERIENCE

Clinicians who decide to work with adolescent sex offenders need training that deals specifically with providing services to this population. That training should be ongoing so that the clinician, upon identifying an area of personal weakness, will seek out qualified supervision or continuing education.

AWARENESS OF VARIOUS THEORIES

This includes the development of theories over time and their current application to adolescent sex offenders.

AWARENESS OF CURRENT KNOWLEDGE
ABOUT ADOLESCENT SEX OFFENDERS

We have included here two exercises that are useful in exploring clinicians' perceptions of adolescent sex offenders.

Perceptions of Offenders Prior to Training. Write a response to each of the following questions:

1. How would you describe an adolescent sex offender (appearance, age, sex, family life)?
2. What causes the adolescent sex offender to commit his or her sexual offenses?
3. What do you think are the common characteristics among adolescent sex offenders?
4. What do you think society's response should be to adolescents who commit sexual offenses?

Clinicians may find it helpful to discuss the answers to these questions with co-workers to become aware of how offenders are perceived. Inaccurate information can then be corrected.

What Should be Done to Adolescent Sex Offenders? Read the following example and then answer the questions.

Situation: Your 15-year-old son has been babysitting for the next door neighbor's 4-year-old daughter for the last year. The police come to your door and tell you that the neighbors and the social services have reported your son for sexually assaulting the 4-year-old.

Questions: What would you do? How would you respond to your son? How would you feel? What would you do about the assault? What would you want to happen to your son?

Responses to this exercise can be compared with the later material on assessment and treatment (see Chapters 5 and 6).

POSITIVE AND NEGATIVE ASPECTS OF ADOLESCENT SEX-OFFENDER WORK

We have highlighted the need for clinicians interested in working with adolescent offenders to be aware of their own issues and to receive special training to work with this population. Two other important areas to consider are the rewards and drawbacks of working with these types of clients.

REWARDS

The positive aspects of working with adolescent sex offenders come from four sources:

1. The professional challenge involved in stretching one's general clinical skills to deal with the confrontation necessary to bring about change in the sex offender's faulty beliefs and coping styles;
2. The awareness that therapeutic work not only helps offenders but prevents future victims;
3. Greater self-understanding arising from the focus upon one's values and emotions; and
4. Close friendships with co-workers due to the need to provide professional and personal support to one another while providing services to adolescent sex offenders.

DRAWBACKS

Adolescent sex offender work is very demanding and stressful. Clinicians are working with clients who attempt to deny, minimize, or rationalize the extent of their problems and who will be resistant to change, thus posing a risk to the community. These factors can lead to "therapist burnout." The National Task Force on Juvenile Sexual Offending (1988) highlighted the need for organizations to be aware of the strain adolescent sex offender work places upon the clinicians. They stated:

> While providing treatment for juvenile sexual offenders, providers are involved in nontraditional approaches, directive and confrontive techniques, and exposure to deviant sexuality and distorted thinking. Systems must be aware of potential emotional/psychological impacts on providers and take steps to protect against or counter negative effects. (p. 30)

Organizations and clinicians working with adolescent sex offenders have to become aware of the emotional impact this type of work has on treatment providers and take steps to prevent burnout from happening.

Clinicians working with adolescent sex offenders must be aware of their own faulty assumptions, must be sensitive to the reality of the work, and must set personal limits. Some faulty assumptions on the part of the therapist that will contribute to burnout are:

- This type of work will not affect me.
- I can work 8 hours a day with offenders and not be bothered.
- My approach is the only way to treat offenders.
- My personal beliefs about sexuality will not affect my work.
- Everyone I work with will stop offending.
- I'm responsible if the offender re-offends.

These faulty beliefs are stressful because they require the therapist to be perfect. More rational counterparts to these statements are:

- In our program we can only work with these types of offenders, and they must meet the following criteria.
- Sex offender work is demanding and stressful. I have to continually monitor myself for signs of burnout.
- I must set limits on clinical time with offenders and have time to work with other types of nonsex-offender clients.
- There are a number of approaches to working with offenders. I can learn from others and they can learn from me.
- My values and beliefs about human sexuality will affect my efforts to help offenders, and I need to be aware of when they do.
- Some offenders will change and others will continue to offend. My job is to provide the best service I can.
- I'm not responsible if the offender re-offends. I'm responsible for providing the best treatment I can.

The reality of working with adolescent sex offenders is that there are usually more clients than the therapist can adequately serve. Therapists who overestimate themselves and try to accommodate all referrals will become physically and psychologically exhausted, lose perspective, and become rigid. They may become focused on numbers of clients seen rather than therapy offered. Time management skills are very important for therapists when working with offenders.

Therapists have to deal with the limits of both their own skills and the resources available within their agency. Facilities and clinicians have to set firm guidelines for the type of offenders they will serve and decide what skills their clinicians will need to provide sex offender-specific treatment. Attempts to provide generic treatment services will lead to frustration for staff and inappropriate treatment for adolescent offenders.

Chapter 5

ASSESSMENT PROCEDURES

The adolescent who commits a sexual offense urgently requires careful psychological assessment. There are four primary goals of this assessment: (a) to provide information to the court, (b) to design an intervention strategy, (c) to make recommendations for placement of the offender, and (d) to begin orienting the youth (and family) to treatment. An accurate evaluation of the adolescent sex offender's functioning must address the emotional, cognitive, intellectual, behavioral, and interpersonal facets of his life.

The adolescent and his family should be made aware of the means by which their responses during the assessment phase assist in the treatment plan. It must be emphasized that the assessment does not serve to establish guilt or innocence. The limits to confidentiality must also be carefully detailed. The approach we have chosen emphasizes the importance of protecting the community. Consequently, we inform the youth and his family that if we receive information suggesting that new sexually aggressive behavior is planned, we will take action to protect the potential victim. Similarly, if we receive new information concerning previously unreported sexual offenses, we will report those offenses to the authorities.

GENERAL CONSIDERATIONS IN ASSESSMENT

A competently conducted sex offender-specific assessment is the key component in developing treatment and placement alternatives. Figure 1 (p. 33) highlights the relationship between assessment and decision making by illustrating the range of treatment and placement alternatives necessary to adequately service this population.

The assessor's role is to collect data that will assist him or her in recommending which service alternatives are apt to be most beneficial.

Sex offender-specific assessments are similar in some ways to general psychological assessments (e.g., personality assessment) but in other ways are unique. Those who have conducted forensic assessments will be familiar with certain features of an adolescent sex offender assessment (e.g., the need to deal with deception). These features all influence the style of the assessment process in any forensic assessment. However, in conducting adolescent sex offender assessments, the assessor must have a thorough knowledge of the various patterns of offending behavior and how they relate to the adolescent sex offender's risk of re-offending and his coping strategies (e.g., minimization, denial).

The assessor will use his or her familiarity with sex offenders and offending behaviors to establish control in the assessment interview and to deal with the qualities common to forensic assessments. Features similar to forensic assessments include the following: (a) Clients are not voluntary; (b) the assessor has a dual responsibility (protection of society as opposed to meeting offenders' needs); (c) special limits to confidentiality exist; and (d) there are legal implications of assessment data. Each of these four features will now be discussed at greater length.

INVOLUNTARY NATURE OF CLIENTS

Adolescent sex offenders are not voluntary clients because they are usually referred by a third party (e.g., courts, police, child protection workers, family members). Offenders present as a special population of resistant clients because they are not only reluctant to discuss the offenses for which they have been charged, but also are likely to have committed other offenses that have not yet been disclosed. The assessor needs to be aware that adolescent sex offenders will tend to minimize the extent and seriousness of their sexual assaults and will not volunteer any information. The assessor must carefully probe the offenses for which the offender has been charged and continually be alert for indicators of other offenses.

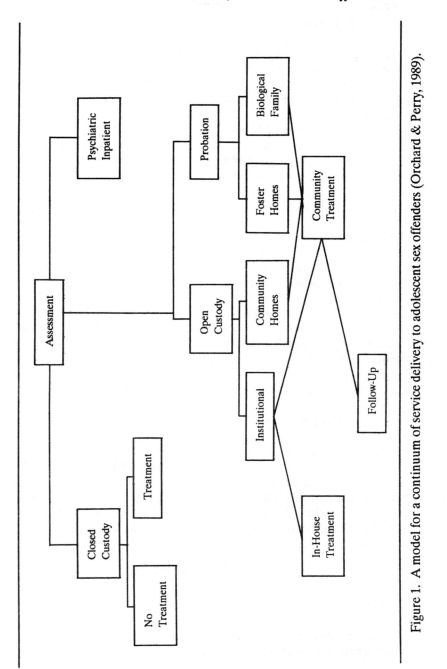

Figure 1. A model for a continuum of service delivery to adolescent sex offenders (Orchard & Perry, 1989).

DUAL RESPONSIBILITY

Adolescent sex offender evaluations serve dual functions: protection of the community and assessment of the treatment needs of the offender. Adolescent sex offenders pose an alarming risk to the community; therefore, protection of society must be considered of paramount importance. The treatment needs of the offender must be addressed within a context that minimizes the risk of re-offending. Often this will mean recommending removal from the biological family; it may also mean recommending stays in correctional facilities.

LIMITS TO CONFIDENTIALITY

Because adolescent sex offenders are referred by a third party, there will be limits on confidentiality. The assessor will share the results of his or her assessment with the court, police, social services, or other referring agencies. Fersch (1980) recommends that involuntary clients being assessed prior to trial be warned of the limits to confidentiality. A psychologist must tell the client that nothing will be held in confidence. In the process of conducting an adolescent sex offender assessment, the assessor may discover that the offender has committed other offenses for which he has not been charged. It is the assessor's duty to inform the referring agency of these offenses.

LEGAL IMPLICATIONS OF ASSESSMENT DATA

Court-ordered assessments require the assessor to provide recommendations for both treatment and sentencing. Figure 1 (p. 33) highlights the importance of providing useful data to courts prior to their making dispositions in order to contribute to sentencing decisions (i.e., closed versus open custody).

ASSESSMENT FORMAT

We have organized the assessment process into seven steps:

1. Information required prior to assessment
2. Overall structure of the assessment
3. Clinical interview of the adolescent sex offender

4. Formal psychological assessment of the adolescent sex offender
5. Clinical interview of the offender's parents
6. Processing of assessment data
7. Generation of a report to the referral source

Each of these will be discussed in turn. This information is designed to guide the clinician in conducting the assessment, summarizing the data, and writing reports for the referring agency or court.

INFORMATION REQUIRED
PRIOR TO ASSESSMENT

Clinical experience has demonstrated the need for access to all existing information concerning the offender and his offenses prior to meeting with him. The offender is not an adequate source of information because he is motivated to conceal facts. The offender's denial and minimization can be challenged by confronting him with conflicting data.

Victims' statements and the offender's statements to police are valuable sources of information with which to corroborate or contradict the offender's current description of the offenses. Bera (1989) reported that the Program for Healthy Adolescent Sexual Expression (PHASE) staff attempt to interview the victims of adolescent sex offenders prior to meeting with the offenders. This contact is maintained, with the victim's consent, throughout the offender's treatment. The offenders are informed by the assessment and treatment staff that these victim contacts will occur. In cases where police have videotaped their interview with the victim of an offender, we have found it useful to observe the tape prior to interviewing the offender.

Other relevant sources of information include previous psychological assessments, educational assessments, social histories, and predisposition reports. These data provide useful information about the offender's past experiences, personality, and intellectual functioning. Such assessments do not specifically address offense patterns, but are still helpful in planning placements and treatment alternatives.

The assessor will feel pressured to respond rapidly to referrals despite inadequate information. We cannot stress strongly enough that time must be taken to collect background information related to offense patterns. At times the assessor will be unable to obtain that information. In the absence of information concerning offenses, the assessor must qualify his or her confidence in the data he or she obtains from the offender. Two methods we have found useful in these types of situations are to interview the parents (together and apart) prior to interviewing the offender, and to take a particularly challenging stance with the offender. Although we offer coping strategies to deal with these situations, we recommend that the assessor attempt to obtain as much relevant information as possible prior to doing the assessment.

OVERALL STRUCTURE OF THE ASSESSMENT

Prior to discussing the assessment process, we will highlight how we generally structure our assessments of adolescent sex offenders:

- *Initial Interview with the Offender.* In the first session the offender is interviewed about offenses (40 to 90 minutes). During this interview we decide if any psychological tests should be administered.
- *Psychological Testing.* If we have decided to test the offender, the next session is devoted to this task. The time required to complete testing varies with each offender and the type and number of tests the assessor decides to administer.
- *Interview with the Offender's Parents.* The parents are interviewed both together and separately. This usually requires two 1-hour sessions.
- *Reinterview of Offender.* After collecting the previous data we generally conduct one or two more interviews with the offender to discuss his offenses and other areas of his life (e.g., school, peer relationships).

This procedure varies depending on the offender and our time constraints.

CLINICAL INTERVIEW OF THE ADOLESCENT SEX OFFENDER

Ross (1988, 1989) and Ross et al. (1988) have stressed that the clinical interview is the most effective assessment tool. Psychological tests complement the information obtained in the interview. The clinical interview serves three purposes: collecting data, educating the offender, and beginning to establish rapport.

Bera (1989) and Groth and Loredo (1981) have pointed out that any given sex offense may cut across all types of conventional diagnostic classifications. The offense itself is not a diagnostic category; it is a behavioral act. The evaluation of the sexually abusive adolescent, then, requires not only that the sex offense be carefully examined but that this behavior be examined in the context of the offender's current lifestyle - particularly his family situation.

Data Collection. The assessment must evaluate all aspects of the adolescent sex offender's life including emotional functioning; cognitive functioning; behavioral functioning; academic/intellectual functioning; social relationships with peers and extrafamilial adults; family relationships; community involvement; substance abuse; delinquent history; history of aggressive behavior; history of victimization (sexual and physical); sexual behaviors and fantasy life; offense pattern; previous treatment; and risk of re-offending.

The assessor will find it useful to follow a structured guide when interviewing the offender; such an approach insures the collection of complete data and establishes the assessor's control over the interview. A sample interview appears in Appendix A (pp. 111-114).

The approach to interviewing must respond to the unique qualities of the adolescent sex offender. The offender's motivation is to maintain control by denying, lying, minimizing, and rationalizing the extent of his inappropriate sexual behaviors. The assessor has to establish that he or she is in charge of the interview and is aware that all attempts by the offender to divert the process represent efforts to take control. We have found that having information from other sources and using a very structured interview allows us to remain focused and to collect the relevant data. The label used by Ross (1989) and Ross et al. (1988) to describe this process is *investigative interviewing*, meaning that the assessor has to be direct, confrontive, and use the offender's anxiety to break down his defenses. The offender must perceive the assessor as an authority figure.

We begin the interview with an explanation of its purpose and limits to confidentiality and a description of our qualifications. The messages to the offender are that (a) we have expertise in assessing and treating adolescent sex offenders and therefore will not be easily manipulated, and that (b) priority will be given to the protection of potential victims. It is important that the assessor present a very confident image to the offender.

Educating the Offender. The educational process begins immediately after the introductions. We inform the offender of the following:

1. Sex offending, like alcoholism, is a lifelong problem.
2. Sex offenses have both immediate and lifelong destructive effects on victims.
3. It is fortunate that the offender has been caught because he will now have to deal with his sexual offending behaviors.
4. The typical pattern of an adolescent sex offender is to vow, after each offense, that he will not re-offend. In reality, without treatment, this pattern of re-offending will continue.
5. The typical defense mechanisms (denial, minimization, lying) of offenders are presented and explained. In this way we predict and therefore gain control over the offender's attempts to sidetrack the assessor (e.g., attempts to change the topic).
6. Despite the protestations of the offender, sexual offenses are not impulsive acts.
7. The focus of therapy will be upon having the offender gain an understanding of his reasons for offending and the circumstances under which he would be at risk of re-offending, and identifying the thinking patterns and behaviors he will have to change.

Establishing Rapport. During the educational process we also work on establishing rapport with the offender. Some clinicians who work with adolescent sex offenders do not give sufficient emphasis to development of rapport, but we have found it to be compatible with an investigative interview style. We attempt to develop rapport by (a) extending an offer of help; (b) making a distinction between the youth as a sex offender and the youth as a person (we explain to the youth that he is a sex offender, but also highlight some of his positive traits that are not related to sex offending); (c) acknowledging that the interview process is anxiety provoking, but at the same time continuing the questioning; and (d) complimenting the offender when he discloses about his offenses.

These techniques can be used throughout the assessment and treatment process to establish rapport.

Content of Clinical Interview. This discussion of the interview follows the outline of the structured interview guide (Appendix A, pp. 111-114).

After we have explained the purpose of the interview we immediately initiate a discussion about the sexual offenses with which the youth has been charged (offenses of record). We make it clear to the offender that we have information concerning his offenses (e.g., victim's statements) and that we will compare the information he provides with those records.

When we first began to work with adolescent sex offenders we focused initially on less threatening topics (e.g., school, friends). However, we discovered that this procedure merely escalated the offender's anxiety and gave the impression that we were not going to discuss the offenses of record. Assessors who are new to the field are tempted to delay discussing the sexual offenses due to their own discomfort.

The next several points relate to the exploration of a sexual offending pattern. We start this process by asking the offender to describe his sexual offenses. We make it clear that we expect him to provide a detailed description of each incident, even those for which he has not been charged. Once the offender has given his initial description we guide further discussion with specific questions (e.g., "What exactly did you do? Did you have her touch your penis - with hands or mouth?").

We are interested in establishing what specific sexual acts the offender committed. Our experience has taught us that the adolescent sex offender will tend to provide minimal and distorted information and must be guided through his descriptions of offenses.

Once we have obtained statements from the offender that are consistent with the victims' statements, we move on to a discussion of the offender's thoughts and feelings during the assaults. The purpose of this line of questioning is to assess the offender's capacity to have empathy for the victim, his sensitivity to his own affect, his level of hostility during offending, and his distorted thinking about his offending behaviors (e.g., many offenders are able to ignore the resistance of their victims by interpreting these actions to mean something other than fear and pain).

This discussion leads into exploration of the offender's thoughts and feelings prior to committing offenses, including the reasons for his choice of victims and circumstances in which to offend. The assessor needs to take time to carefully explore these areas because it is important to know the thinking and fantasizing that culminate in offending. The crucial questions to ask are:

- What made you choose this victim or these victims?
- How did you set up the circumstances to offend?
- What kinds of things did you say to yourself to try to convince yourself that you would not offend?
- Once you decided to commit the offense, what excuses did you create for your behavior?
- What sexual acts did you think of doing to your victim prior to your offenses?
- Why didn't you act on all those thoughts? *or* What made you do more?

The area we explore next is the offender's behaviors, thoughts, and feelings after the offenses to ascertain how the offender rationalized and justified his behaviors. It is common for the adolescent sex offender to tell himself that he will never re-offend. In reality, the offender will continue to make these kinds of statements after each new offense. The following questions will assist the assessor:

- What did you get out of the offense?
- How did you feel after the offense?
- What did you say to yourself?
- What did you say or do to the victim after the offense?
- How did you convince the victim not to tell?
- Did you do anything to try to prevent future offenses?
- What other sexual assaults have you committed?
- What do you think contributed to your re-offending?

Adolescent sexual offenses are not purely sexual acts, but also meet needs for power and control. The assessor must not be deceived into thinking that sexual gratification was the sole motive for offending. Levels of aggression in the offender's behaviors, thoughts, and fantasies must be explored. It is useful to ask offenders who were aggressive toward their victims: What stopped you from hurting the victim more (i.e., killing)? For those offenders who did not use aggression in their sexual assaults: What stopped you from using physical force against your victim?

After collecting all the preceding information it is important to assess the offender's attitudes toward his victims. Developing empathy for his victims is one of the major obstacles to re-offending. Indicators of the offender's capacity for empathy include (a) the extent to which he blames the victims (e.g., "She seduced me"; "She wanted me"; "She asked for it"; "She enjoyed it"); (b) the use of demeaning terms to describe his victims (e.g., bitch, slut); and (c) failure to recognize the effects of the assaults on his victims, both short-term and long-term (e.g., "The assaults didn't seem to bother her"; "She still talks to me").

By this stage of the assessment, the assessor should be able to evaluate the offender on the following dimensions:

1. Acceptance of responsibility for offenses
2. Extent of empathy for victim
3. Offense pattern (i.e., selection of victims, planning of offenses)
4. Level of aggression (behaviors and fantasies)
5. Escalation in severity or frequency of offending
6. Extent of denial, minimization, and rationalization
7. Deviant values and thoughts
8. Mood
9. Intellectual ability

At this point in the interview the focus shifts to the offender's victimization. We place the exploration of the offender's victimization experiences after a thorough examination of his offenses in order to emphasize the offender's responsibility.

Traditionally, assessments have focused upon sexual victimization. Both our review of the literature and our clinical experience have highlighted the need to broaden the meaning of abuse to include physical, emotional, and sexual victimization. For example, Davis and Leitenberg (1987) found that of all the clinical impressions about the backgrounds of adolescent sex offenders, only a history of physical abuse could be substantiated. Therefore, the assessor needs to conduct a thorough evaluation of the offender's past to uncover any indications of abuse of any kind. Offenders are often reluctant to disclose having been abused and also may not correctly label certain experiences as abusive. The assessor needs to give the offender a number of examples of what might be defined as abusive (e.g., "Has anyone ever hit you when you did something wrong or even when you did not? Who? What happened?" "Has anyone ever touched you in your private areas? Who? What did he or she do?"). When a history of victimization is presented, this may contribute to the offender's assaultive behaviors; but it must be made clear to the offender that he is still responsible for committing his offenses.

Sexuality is the next area we focus upon by examining the offender's knowledge and experience. We are interested in assessing basic sexual knowledge (e.g., masturbation), attitudes toward sexual intimacy, deviant sexual values (e.g., it is acceptable to demand sex from anyone less powerful than you), stimuli that are arousing (e.g., pornography), fantasies, and actual sexual experience (e.g., first sexual experience). This information provides some insight into deviant sexual arousal patterns. Some sample questions are:

- Tell me about your sexual fantasies. (Start with the general question, then move to more specific questions about the victim or others.)
- How old were you when you started to masturbate?
- How often do you masturbate?
- What do you think about when you are masturbating?
- What was your first sexual experience?

During the interview process, the assessor must carefully monitor the adolescent sex offender for any signs of suicidal ideation. Some offenders pose a high risk of suicide because they are closer in age to the time of their own victimization. If the assessor observes any signs that the offender is contemplating suicide, he or she must act to prevent the offender from acting on those impulses.

The remaining areas of assessment focus upon social and community functioning: family, peer relationships, recreation, school, and substance abuse and other delinquent activities. This information provides a global perspective of the strengths and weaknesses in the offender's life that will be used in assessing prognosis, placement, and treatment. We provide a number of questions in our structured interview guide that will assist the assessor in collecting this information.

Ross (1989) points out that the three most common mistakes made by assessors when they interview adolescent sex offenders are:

1. *The assessor loses control of the interview and allows the offender to take control.* Once in charge, the offender will avoid discussing his offenses. The assessor loses control for a variety of reasons: fear of the offender; absence of accurate corroborative data about the offender's assaults prior to the interview; discomfort in discussing sexual or offense-specific issues; hostility toward the offender; pity for the offender; lack of confidence; or lack of training to carry out the interview. For example, in one case in which we were involved as supervisors, a female therapist became intimidated during her initial assessment session, both by the description of the offender's assaults (violent rape) and by his actions during the interview. The offender took control by using a variety of nonverbal techniques to intimidate the interviewer (e.g., eyeing her when he talked about raping his victim). She became anxious and ended the interview.

   To combat the offender's attempts to gain control, we helped the therapist organize a very structured approach to handling the assessment. At the beginning of the next interview, she took a very confrontive stance. She told him she would not tolerate any attempts to be abusive to her. Her statements were presented as statements of fact and did not require the offender to respond. Then she told him that the assessment would involve him being interviewed and completing a variety of tests. She would tell him what to do, and if she felt he was not being cooperative or was trying to control the interview, she would end the assessment and inform the court of his actions. If she began to feel uncomfortable with the offender, she would direct him to complete a written task (e.g., psychological). This strategy placed her in total control because the offender could not predict what was going to happen next. It also allowed her to take breaks without letting the offender realize he was getting to her. She was in control and gained a great deal of valuable information about the offender and his offenses.

   The assessor should do everything possible to insure that he or she is in control of the interview. We have found it useful to have more than one person designated as the sex offender worker. This provides workers with other clinicians who can be supportive and also give consultation.

2. *The assessor assumes he or she has an answer to a question instead of exploring in more detail.* Adolescent offenders will supply the assessor with minimal information to his or her prompts. The assessor must repeat the same questions a number of times and explore the offender's answers. He or she must not accept answers such as "I forget," "I can't remember," "I only touched her once," and so forth. Numerous factors within the assessor may contribute to his or her assumptions (e.g., lack of training, frustration with the offender's response style, etc.).

    The assessor must continually explore and challenge the offender's responses and style of responding. For example, in one case the offender kept responding to our questions about his assaults by providing minimal information or by stating "I can't remember; I have a poor memory; it was so long ago that this is all I can remember." Based on reports we received from other people who had interviewed this offender, this strategy had been successful for him, resulting in almost no available information on the exact nature of his offenses. We felt that no one had confronted him with his actions. We stopped the interview and told the offender that his style of responding was not going to work, and that if he continued to respond in this manner we would take this as a sign of his being a dangerous offender. We would then inform the court about our findings. We left the room for 5 minutes, came back, and restarted the interview. He was more cooperative and suddenly experienced a recovery of his memory.

    Offenders use a variety of verbal (e.g., "I forget; I only did this") and nonverbal (e.g., crying, raising the voice) behaviors to supply minimal information. The assessor has to take a very explorative approach and not allow himself or herself to get distracted and make assumptions about an offender's actions.

3. *Assessors take sides by becoming either punitive or allied with the offender.* Some clinicians feel sorry for an offender when they find out that he has been sexually abused. The more severe the abuse, the more pity they have for the offender and the less responsible they feel he is for his assaults. Other clinicians respond to adolescent sex offenders as though they have some type of very contagious disease, and want to have them locked up.

We have found that the most useful strategy is to maintain neutrality by receiving extensive training in sex offender theory and assessment procedures; understanding the dual role (protection of society and treatment of the offender) of the assessment; and having a colleague with whom to consult.

FORMAL PSYCHOLOGICAL TESTING OF THE OFFENDER

Over the course of conducting the interview, the assessor may generate questions concerning the intelligence, academic functioning, level of depression, delinquent ideation, clarity of thought processes, social skills, and family dynamics of the adolescent sex offender. Among various psychological tests the assessor may administer, the following may be particularly useful.

Jesness Inventory. This contains 155 true/false items and was designed for use in the classification and treatment of disturbed children and adolescents, primarily delinquents. It provides scores on 11 personality characteristics (e.g., social maladjustment, immaturity, manifest aggression, withdrawal-depression, denial). Special templates can also be used to classify the adolescent into one or more of the 9 I-level Subtypes (e.g., unsocialized-aggressive, neurotic-acting out). *Contact:* Multi-Health Systems, Inc., 908 Niagara Falls Boulevard, North Tonawanda, NY 14120-2060. Telephone: 1-800-456-3003.

Jesness Behavior Checklist. This instrument consists of 80 items that measure 14 bipolar behavioral factors (e.g., responsibility versus irresponsibility, anger control versus hypersensitivity). The adolescent has to read each statement and decide whether he has behaved in the stated manner very often, fairly often, sometimes, not often, or almost never. An equivalent Observer Form is also available, which allows an adult who has known the youth to rate his behaviors along the same dimensions. This procedure allows the evaluator to compare the adolescent's self-ratings with those made by others. *Contact:* Multi-Health Systems, Inc., 908 Niagara Falls Boulevard, North Tonawanda, NY 14120-2060. Telephone: 1-800-456-3003.

Family Assessment Measure (FAM). This self-report instrument provides quantitative indices of family strengths and weaknesses. It consists of three components: (a) a General Scale, which focuses on the family as a system; (b) a Dyadic Relationship Scale, which examines relationships between specific pairs within the family (e.g., father-mother); and (c) a Self-Rating Scale. This scale taps the individual's perceptions of his functioning within the family. *Contact:* Multi-Health Systems, Inc., 908 Niagara Falls Boulevard, North Tonawanda, NY 14120-2060. Telephone: 1-800-456-3003.

Raven's Standard Progressive Matrices. This is a self-report instrument that provides a nonverbal culture-fair measure of intellectual abilities. *Contact:* H. K. Lewis & Co. Ltd., 136 Gower Street, London, England W.C.1, or in the U.S. contact The Psychological Corporation, Order Service Center, P.O. Box 839954, San Antonio, TX 78283-3954. Telephone: 1-800-228-0752, or outside U.S. call 512-299-1061.

Sex Knowledge History. A useful method of assessing the adolescent's general sexual knowledge and experience is to ask him direct questions related to the issues listed on page 42. This strategy was introduced to us by Ms. Emily Coleman. Contact the authors for additional information.

Wechsler Intelligence Scale for Children - Third Edition (WISC-III). This instrument assesses mental ability in children. It is composed of 13 subtests divided into Verbal (e.g., Information, Vocabulary) and Performance (e.g., Block Design, Picture Completion) Scales. This test yields a Verbal IQ, a Performance IQ, and a Full Scale IQ for children tested individually. It provides scaled scores between the ages of 6-0 and 16-11 years. The test data can also be used as possible aids in psychiatric diagnosis. *Contact:* The Psychological Corporation, Order Service Center, P.O. Box 839954, San Antonio, TX 78283-3954. Telephone: 1-800-228-0752, or outside U.S. call 512-299-1061.

Wechsler Adult Intelligence Scale - Revised (WAIS-R). This instrument assesses intelligence in adolescents and adults. Normative sample consisted of 1,800 cases including an equal number of men and women distributed over nine age levels: 16-17 to 70-74. It is composed of 11 subtests. Six subtests are included in the Verbal Scale (e.g., Information, Vocabulary) and five in the Performance Scale (e.g., Picture Completion, Block Design). The test provides three measures of intelligence

(Verbal, Performance, and Full Scale). The test data can also be used as possible aids in psychiatric diagnosis. *Contact:* The Psychological Corporation, Order Service Center, P.O. Box 839954, San Antonio, TX 78283-3954. Telephone: 1-800-228-0752, or outside U.S. call 512-299-1061.

CLINICAL INTERVIEW OF THE OFFENDER'S PARENTS

It is imperative that the parents or significant care givers (e.g., foster parents) of the adolescent sex offender be interviewed as part of the assessment process. Paralleling the clinical interview of the offender, the parental interview serves three purposes: to begin to establish rapport, to educate, and to collect data. Decisions with regard to placement of the offender will be influenced by the relationship between the victim and the offender (i.e., incest offenders versus extrafamilial). Offenders who have abused a nuclear family member will have to be removed from the home. The task of the assessor is to judge the parents' willingness to support treatment even when it means making painful choices such as having their son removed from their home.

In the ensuing discussion we refer to parents; however, the same basic approach to assessment can be used with single parent families and foster parents. When interviewing single parents or blended families, however, the assessor needs to collect information on the absent biological parent.

Rapport Building. Therapy begins with the assessment process because from the outset the task of the assessor is to establish a working relationship with the parents. Begin this by explaining to the parents that your role is to join with them to help their son change a serious problem. It is important to emphasize to the parents that you have expertise in working with adolescent sex offenders; this establishes your credibility and stresses the gravity of the offending behavior. The parents will feel reassured upon hearing your qualifications and will also be less likely to try to deceive you. Rapport building continues throughout the assessment process.

Education. The parents come to the assessment interview with minimal understanding of sexual offending behavior and numerous misperceptions. They subscribe to many of the myths outlined earlier and thus try to minimize the severity of their son's behavior. Exploring the parents' belief system concerning the sexual offenses is useful for gauging how supportive the parents will be to the therapeutic process and for guiding the educational process. The assessor needs to provide information about the following topics: psychology of the offender, victimization, role of the parents in providing supervision, and the treatment contract. Ross et al. (1988) have developed an excellent curriculum that can be used to educate both parents and offenders.

Data Collection. The following features of family functioning need to be assessed:

1. Parents' perceptions of the sexual offenses
2. Parental description of offender's overall functioning (e.g., school, sibling relationships)
3. Co-parenting roles (i.e., role of each parent in the family)
4. Marital relationship
5. History of abuse (physical and sexual) within nuclear and extended family
6. Substance abuse within the family
7. Parents' attitudes toward therapy

Content of Clinical Interview. A sample interview for the parents (Appendix B) is provided on pages 115-118. As with the offender interview, we begin by focusing on the sexual offending behaviors. The assessor's goal is to obtain a detailed understanding of what the parents believe happened and their attitudes toward their son's actions. The extent to which the parents minimize and justify his sexual assaults will influence their willingness to monitor their son in the community and his compliance with treatment. A common treatment stipulation is that the offender not be allowed to babysit. If the offender is living in the home, it is the parents who must enforce this rule.

The next phase of the interview involves the exploration of a history of sexual, physical, or substance abuse within the immediate and extended families. When exploring sexual abuse, the following factors need to be considered:

1. Is this a family of multigenerational abuse?
2. If there have been other incidents of abuse within the nuclear or extended family, how were they dealt with?

Has the family kept it to themselves or did they receive treatment? The parents' style of handling earlier abuse will influence how they deal with their son's offenses.

3. A history of sexual victimization or offending by either parent may affect how he or she will interact with the son as an offender.

4. When the adolescent has abused a family member, the parents are called upon to protect the victim. Their ability to do so will be influenced by their past histories of victimization or offending behaviors.

5. If the assessor suspects ongoing sexual abuse is occurring within the family, protection of all the children, including the offender, becomes a priority.

Families of offenders often have a history of physical abuse (Davis & Leitenberg, 1987). Indicators of physical abuse can be sought by assessing how the parents discipline their children, handle marital conflicts, and express anger. Having grown up in a physically abusive family will affect how the offender deals with his own anger and with issues of power and control.

Parental lifestyle also has an impact on the offender. Factors to explore are substance abuse, social network, and work history. In families where there is chronic substance abuse, the parents' abilities to deal with the sexual abuse are severely impaired (e.g., parents cannot enforce limits on the offender). Socially isolated families tend to produce children who have low self-esteem and limited social skills, and who are less likely to reach out into the community for help.

Parents are also excellent sources of information about the social, community, and school functioning of the offender. The assessor can use this material to corroborate the offender's statements, to evaluate the parents' involvement with the offender (e.g., "Is one parent more attached to the offender than the other parent?"), and to assess the parents' opinions and feelings toward their son (e.g., "Do they think he is a success/okay/a loser?").

Throughout the course of therapy the parents will continually be required to assume an authoritative role. The assessor needs to ascertain who has been the main parenting figure, how the parents interact when they parent their children, how they discipline, and how they encourage and motivate their children to improve.

As we assess the family relationships we are also assessing the marital relationship. How do the parents interact with each other? How do they deal with disagreements? What is the power balance? These data can be obtained by interviewing the parents together or separately.

Throughout the assessment interview with the parents, the assessor will receive information about the parents' openness to treatment. Their willingness to become involved in treatment is one of the variables that may determine placement of the offender.

RISK ASSESSMENT

One of the assessor's central tasks is to assess the offender's risk of re-offending. Several experts in the field have put forward frameworks for this (Bengis, 1986; Dreiblatt, 1982; Groth, 1977; Perry & Orchard, 1989; Wenet & Clark, 1983). We have provided a sample checklist (Appendix C, pp. 119-122) which emphasizes several key factors in the assessment of risk. The characteristics included in our checklist below are grouped into those concerning the offender, and those concerning his family/parents.

Offender Characteristics

1. Extent of denial
2. Degree of aggression
3. Range and number of sexual offenses
4. Number, age, and sex of victims
5. Awareness of impact of assaults on victims
6. Previous treatment for sexual offending
7. Past history of physical and/or sexual abuse
8. Level of cooperation with assessment process
9. Motivation for treatment
10. History of other delinquency
11. History of substance abuse
12. Peer relationships and social skills
13. Level of community adjustment (e.g., school)
14. Thought disorder

Family/Parents Characteristics

1. Parental attitudes toward son's offenses (i.e., denial, minimization)

2. Level of involvement with their son
3. Parenting ability
4. Health of marital relationship
5. History of or ongoing physical and/or sexual abuse
6. Parental substance abuse
7. Community adjustment of the family
8. Parental attitudes toward therapy

We use this checklist in organizing our assessment data and thoughts on the offender to make judgments about the offender's potential risk of re-offending if placed in an unsupervised setting. The examiner's risk assessment will affect his or her recommendations for placement and treatment.

Placement and Treatment Recommendations. We have created a Risk Factor Constellation (Appendix D, pp. 123-125) which categorizes the risk factors highlighted by the Risk Checklist. Within this Risk Factor Constellation we have grouped risk factors according to what we believe are the most appropriate placement and treatment services.

Bengis (1986), Perry and Orchard (1989), and Orchard and Perry (1989) have stated that correctional and treatment agencies need to provide a variety of placement and treatment alternatives for adolescent sex offenders. We have outlined our suggestions as a continuum-of-service model for adolescent sex offenders that describes key factors in placement and treatment.

The examiner collects all the relevant information, makes judgments about risk of re-offending, is aware of existing placement and treatment options, and then formulates a plan.

THE ASSESSMENT REPORT

The data collected by the clinician during the assessment process must be integrated into a report that answers several central questions: What is the potential for this youth to re-offend? Is the offender a good candidate for treatment? Where should he be retained (e.g., correctional center, group home, etc.)? When interpreting the results of assessment, some questions may be unanswerable. Dreiblatt (1982) indicates that examiners should avoid assertions that cannot be reasonably justified and substantiated.

Questions

What is the Potential for This Youth to Re-Offend? This question is designed to prompt the examiner's decision as to whether the offender is a low or high risk. The examiner must develop some method for integrating available data to make this assessment. The Risk Checklist and Risk Factor Constellation we have proposed can help the assessor ascertain whether he or she has gathered all the necessary information to make meaningful statements about the offender's likelihood of committing another sexual assault.

The focus of the Risk Factor Constellation is upon the past (immediate and long-term) behaviors of the sex offender. Clinical experience has indicated that key patterns of offending behavior, as well as various other indicators of behavioral, emotional, and familial disturbance, can be used to predict risk of future sexual assaults. Should the adolescent be placed in a closed setting while receiving therapy, or can he be placed in an open community setting and attend outpatient treatment? The clinician should be conservative in judging risk. Key factors include the degree of aggression involved in the offense, the frequency of offending behavior, the degree of arousal to sexually deviant stimuli, tolerance for confrontation, criminal history, other addictive behaviors, and the degree of support and control available from significant others in the home environment.

Is the Offender a Good Candidate for Treatment? The examiner needs to determine if the offender will respond to treatment. Not all sexual offenders respond to treatment, and those denying the offense even after conviction are poor candidates. In making this decision, the examiner should assess the individual, his family, and his environmental resources. Individual considerations include motivation for treatment, rigidity of ego defenses, and internal resources. The offender's parents need to recognize that their son's actions were morally and legally wrong. They must be willing to set limits on his behavior and to participate in therapy.

If the family of the offender is unwilling to support treatment, the decision on treatment will be based upon the willingness of the court to remove the youth from the home. If the offender admits to the charges and appears somewhat motivated to receive therapy, he should be placed out of the home to receive treatment. If such a placement is not possible, the success of therapy is likely to be minimized by the family's resistance. It is also useless to make treatment recommendations when there is no facility in the region that offers these services.

Some clinicians have difficulty making the recommendation for no treatment. It is important to realize that in some cases inappropriate treatment recommendations are harmful to both the offender and society. Frances, Clarkin, and Perry (1984) suggest some benefits that may follow from a no-treatment decision:

1. Avoiding a semblance of treatment when no effective treatment exists
2. Delaying treatment until a more appropriate time
3. Protecting the patient and the clinician from wasting time, effort, and money

Where Should the Offender Be Retained? The type of residential placement judged to be appropriate will vary according to the sex offender's performance on the Risk Factor Constellation. The assessor must respond to a highly controversial question: Can the offender remain in the community? In responding, the clinician should consider what is best for society as well as for the offender. High-risk offenders need to be located in centers where adequate controls can be placed on antisocial behaviors. The offender who behaves in any of the following ways should be placed in a locked correctional setting while receiving in-house treatment (Orchard & Perry, 1989; Smith, 1985):

1. Acknowledges his offenses but is violent
2. Has offended against multiple victims
3. Has shown disregard for victims' distress
4. Has shown an escalation in the frequency of offenses, or in the type or level of aggression
5. Is highly delinquent
6. Has received community-based treatment but has continued to offend
7. Has no family or community support network (e.g., has a family that is very dysfunctional and/or is unsupportive of treatment)

In most instances, residence in the community while receiving treatment is appropriate when (a) sexual offenders are nonviolent; (b) the sexual activity did not involve any bizarre or ritualistic interpersonal acts (e.g., bondage); (c) the sexual offense is a first offense with no history of chronic antisocial or violent behavior; (d) there is no evidence of any serious psychopathology; (e) the offender acknowledges his offense and is motivated for treatment, and there is a dependable agent to monitor and supervise his daily living; (f) the offender has competent social, intellectual, and psychological resources and skills to manage his life; and (g) there are dependable treatment and support services available in the community.

The Report. After the clinician has accumulated all the previous information, he or she must organize and present it in a way that is useful to the court or other referring agencies. We suggest the following report format:

1. Clinical Interview of the Youth
   a. Details of the offense (age difference of victim/offender, relationship between the two, type of sexual act, use of coercion, violence)
   b. History of other sexual offenses
   c. Sexual history, including sexual fantasies
   d. Victimization experiences
   e. Personal interests/strengths
   f. Family relationships (areas of support/weaknesses)
   g. Peer relationships
   h. Intellectual and personality assessment
2. Interview of Parents
   a. Parental response to sexual offense
   b. Functioning of the couple as co-parents
   c. Status of the marital relationship
3. Statement on Risk Posed to the Community
4. Summary and Recommendations

A sample report follows on pages 55-61.

PSYCHOLOGICAL ASSESSMENT

IDENTIFICATION

Client: Andy
Age: 15 years
Family: Lives with biological parents and younger brother (8 years old) and sister (5 years old)

REASON FOR REFERRAL

Andy was referred for a psychological assessment by the court. He had entered a guilty plea to sexually assaulting two younger children. The purpose of this assessment was to provide information to the court which would assist in determining the sentence. The data in this report were gathered from:

1. contact with the offender and his family (two meetings with Andy, one meeting with Andy's parents, a family meeting, and three psychological tests administered to Andy and/or his parents), and
2. reading the victim's statements and talking with the arresting officer.

DETAILS OF SEXUAL ASSAULT

Andy had sexually assaulted two younger children. In both cases the assaults involved manipulating the victim into performing various sexual acts (fondling, oral and anal sex) and then telling the victim that he or she would get into trouble if he or she told. His victims were:

1. A male cousin whom he sexually molested over a 2-year period. Andy began to assault the boy when he was 3 years old.
2. A 6-year-old girl. Andy molested her while babysitting her on five different occasions. In both cases, he started with touching, then progressed to oral and anal sexual activities.

When we first questioned Andy about the charges, he stated that he had only touched them and had done nothing else. We informed him that we had talked with the police and had read the victims' statements; attempts to deny what he had done would get him into more trouble. He then admitted to the other sexual activities.

When we asked Andy if he masturbated, he initially denied that he would do this. After we explained that most adolescents his age did so, he reported that he masturbated. During our discussion of the assaults and what aroused Andy, we discovered that his sexual fantasies involved thinking and fantasizing about his sexual assaults on his victims.

Andy reported that he learned about sex when he was 10 years old. He had an older friend who told him about sex and his sexual relationships with his girlfriend. When he was 12 he remembered watching some pornographic movies that graphically depicted a variety of male/female sexual acts. Andy reported that he had never been sexually abused.

INTERVIEW WITH PARENTS

The parents were unsure how to react to Andy's sexual offenses. He had a long history of acting-out behaviors (i.e., being aggressive in school), and the parents were uncertain how to separate the sexual offenses from his other problems. At one level, they felt they were dealing with the assaults (i.e., they had talks with him about his inappropriate sexual activities); but at another level, they felt very confused and worried about his assaults. We informed them that they needed to take his sexual assaults very seriously, we provided them with some general information on adolescent sex offenders, and we explained how it related to Andy.

Andy's past acting-out behaviors and current sexual offenses have driven a wedge between his parents. The father seems to cope by denying the severity of the sexual problems. When presented with data he cannot deny, he is capable of confronting Andy, but he seems to believe that once the issue has been confronted it is dealt with. He then moves back into a denial stage.

A possible contributing factor to this style of coping may be a lack of knowledge of how else to handle this problem. The mother has been aware of the problem, but over time has begun to mistrust her perceptions, seeming to feel that she is overreacting and becoming unsure of when or how to react to Andy's offenses. The result is that both parents have begun to mistrust themselves and each other. They are not able to work as a team and their individual efforts virtually cancel out each other's attempts to deal with the situation. They are left frustrated and with a sense of being trapped in an impossible situation.

The parents needed to agree to accept the seriousness of the present problem and commit themselves to focus on the present rather than regretting the past. The parents also reported that they were having trouble living together and had talked about separating. They had stayed together for the children. They had received no counseling for their marital problems.

TEST RESULTS

Intellectual

Andy was administered the Raven's Standard Progressive Matrices. He was found to be functioning within the Average range on this nonverbal, culture-fair instrument of intellectual abilities.

Personality

The following personality characteristics were generated from Andy's responses on the Jesness Inventory:

1. He perceives himself as less adequate than others.
2. He rarely admits to problems.
3. He tends to behave in a somewhat unpredictable fashion.
4. Andy has limited social contacts.
5. He appears fearful and passive, and seeks approval for his behaviors. This is difficult for Andy to achieve because he has a limited social-support network.
6. His formula for bringing about desired change is surface conformity.
7. Anxiety seems to result from rejection by significant adults and peers and from situations that produce uncertainty.
8. Crises are handled through psychological withdrawal, running, or intoxication.
9. Delinquent activities seem to be a way of gaining approval from peers.

Family

Our overall interpretations of the Family Assessment Measure are as follows:

1. Strong indications exist that there are family problems that are perceived very differently by various family members.
2. Both parents reported a lack of affective involvement in the family, which indicates a lack of emotional expression between family members. Andy did not point this out as a problem.
3. Andy pointed out that he saw his parents as too controlling. Everything else was rated in the average range. His responses did not seem to reflect the current problems he is facing at home, and could reflect a denial of problems.

4. Both parents rated Andy as having numerous problems. However, the father did report that Andy had some positive qualities (e.g., good communication skills).
5. Andy's mother did not rate herself as having any major problems in the family, but wrote a number of qualifying responses to her answers.
6. Both spouses noted no problems in interacting with each other. Neither reported problems with the relationship or noted any real strengths. This is an interesting finding in light of the personal problems the parents had reported about their relationship.

RISK ASSESSMENT

We have summarized the data gathered on Andy below, under high and low risk factors for re-offending.

RISK FACTORS

<table>
<tr><th>High Risk</th><th>Low Risk</th></tr>
<tr><td>

- Multiple assaults on various victims
- Victims included both males and females
- Victims varied in age
- Victims included family and nonfamily individuals
- Compulsive ideation
- Broad range of sexual misconduct
- Escalation of sexual offending
- Past history of problems with aggressive acting-out
- Delinquent history
- Numerous personal problems (e.g., poor communication skills)
- Tends to be a loner and the friends he has appear to be low functioning
- Limited social outlets for enjoyment

</td><td>

- Passive offender
- Used manipulation
- No previous treatment for sexual offending
- No history of substance abuse
- Does not blame victims for assaults

</td></tr>
</table>

RISK FACTORS *(Continued)*

<u>High Risk</u>   <u>Low Risk</u>

- Problems in school
- Seems to have difficulty processing that his assaults are wrong and harmful to others, especially his victims
- Resistant to taking responsibility for his inappropriate sexual activity
- Had trouble discussing his assaults
- Became emotional during assessment, but distress seemed to be related to his fears about going to jail and did not appear to be generated by remorse for victims
- Family problems, parental marital problems
- Parents are not able to control youth's actions

The preceding data strongly suggest that Andy is at high risk for re-offending. The most telling factors are multiple victims, escalating offenses, minimization of effects on victim, and limited cognitive awareness of self and others' needs and feelings. There are few factors that indicate that he is a low risk. In addition to the factors mentioned previously, Andy's sexual fantasies revolve around his acting-out behavior. He reported to us that he masturbates to fantasies and thoughts about previous inappropriate sexual activities. In addition, his parents cannot control him, and placement outside the home must be considered.

<u>SUMMARY</u>

Andy's current style of functioning and previous history make him a high risk for re-offending. He needs to receive specialized sex offender-specific treatment and should be placed in an environment that places strong controls on his behaviors but, at the same time, also provides stimulation for change. However, prior to receiving any type of therapy, Andy needs to participate in training that will help him learn general (e.g., verbal) skills he can use in therapy to help him deal with his sexually offending behaviors.

RECOMMENDATIONS

1. Andy needs to receive a strong message from the court that his sexually offending behaviors are inappropriate. We recommend a period of open custody and a long probation. These conditions will place strong external controls on Andy which the treatment and social services staff can use to maintain him in an appropriate treatment program.

2. Andy needs to reside in an environment that places strong controls on him, but is also conducive to personal growth. Placement in a correctional center would have long-term negative effects on Andy and the community. We suggest placement in an open-custody community home. This type of environment would place the necessary controls on his movement yet also allow him to live in a more home-like environment, and would not expose him to as many delinquent youths.

3. The treatment program has a number of components:

   a. Pre-sex-offender treatment training. Andy needs to learn a vocabulary and basic communication skills to help him identify and describe his feelings and thoughts.

   b. Once the above skills have been learned, Andy can begin a sex offender-specific treatment program involving individual, group, and, possibly, family therapy. Placing Andy in a treatment program without having him develop the above skills would likely meet with limited results because the therapeutic process relies on verbal interactions, introspection, and cognitive restructuring. These components of therapy can only be achieved when Andy has the verbal and cognitive skills to function in therapy.

   c. After therapy is completed, Andy will need long-term follow-up contacts to insure he is not regressing.

4. To facilitate all the preceding recommendations, Andy needs to have a one-on-one worker who has time to meet with him on a regular basis. The one-on-one worker could serve as a case manager, insuring that Andy fulfills all the requirements of his treatment and placement.

5. Andy should not be allowed to associate with young children until he has been involved in sex offender-specific treatment. Younger children are his targets for sexual assault and he

should not be provided with the opportunity to commit an offense.

6. Prior to Andy returning home, he and his parents should become involved in family therapy. The parents need to learn how to manage him and he needs to learn how to express his needs within the family.
7. The parents would benefit from marital therapy.

_____   _____
(Clinician's Name and Title)   (Date)

cc: (We note on the report who receives copies of the report.)

 Chapter 6

TREATMENT

GENERAL CONSIDERATIONS

In this chapter we will review the various treatment options available to clinicians and administrators when planning treatment programs for adolescent sex offenders.

The adolescent sex offender's motivation is to mislead the clinician so that the offender can appear to cooperate with treatment while not being forced to confront difficult topics such as his offense pattern. The offender may also tend to miss treatment sessions or attend but not participate. We have stressed that sex offenders most often do not present as voluntary clients. Instead, they arrive for assessment and treatment under duress. Thus, the clinician cannot rely on the sex offender's internal motivation to be helped in order to obtain his cooperation. Perhaps later in treatment this will be possible, but certainly not in the early or even middle stages of therapy.

Treatment must be mandated by the court to be effective. The court order provides a backup for the therapeutic process. Therapists can use the legal system as leverage to motivate the youth's continued cooperation with treatment.

The adolescent sex offender tends to be unlike other delinquent groups. He may present as cooperative, compliant, and agreeable; a "nice boy." Too often the therapist is convinced by the youth that his sexual offense was a momentary aberration which will not recur. This represents one of the most dangerous mythical beliefs about adolescent sex offenders. That pleasant, seemingly remorseful young man is at risk of committing another sexual offense.

The sexual offenses must be confronted directly in the treatment sessions. The offenses *cannot* be ignored, avoided, or minimized. Treatment must help the offender to (a) understand the compulsive nature of his offense and develop internal and external controls on his behavior; (b) alter his attitudes and beliefs that support the pathology. He has to admit to his offense and accept responsibility for his actions. Part of this responsibility entails finding some way of making restitution for what he has done; (c) become aware that his sexual preference is considered illegal and deviant by society. He must learn more appropriate sexual preferences; and (d) find ways of coping with stress and develop behavioral management skills to deal with life's demands (e.g., assertiveness skills).

To accomplish the above, treatment will likely encompass a combination of reeducation, resocialization, individual psychotherapy, and family therapy.

Clinicians must be able to confront the client and identify the behaviors that must cease. To accomplish this, it is necessary to (a) feel comfortable giving orders to the offender; (b) set limits and boundaries for the offender; (c) define and enforce sanctions on the offender; (d) demand responsible behavior from the offender; (e) use court leverage to control the offender; and (f) do all of the above *plus* convey a level of concern for the offender as a person - no matter how stringent the sanctions.

Treatment should be broken down into distinct stages, each with a specific focus and reasonable duration. This process will allow for immediate feedback and reinforcement from the therapist, and is also suited to the short attention span and low frustration tolerance of adolescents. Smets and Cebula (1987) and Breer (1987) present five-step group therapy programs for adolescent sex offenders. Smets and Cebula's (1987) model carefully describes the progress each youth must make from initial denial and resistance to the development of a restitution plan, along with a coping strategy to break the offense cycle.

TREATMENT ISSUES

A variety of treatment issues need to be considered when planning an adolescent sex offender treatment program. Treatment issues may be grouped around the following five broad goals:

1. Helping adolescents to assume responsibility for their offenses by challenging the rationalizations, denials, and minimizations upon which offenders rely to avoid assuming responsibility.
2. Helping adolescent sex offenders to develop empathy for the experience of their victims and a more comprehensive emotional awareness in all aspects of their lives.
3. Assisting offenders in achieving a more complete understanding of their own individual offense pattern, and working with them to develop strategies to use if they find themselves once again beginning the cycle leading to offending behavior.
4. Providing new information to challenge their very rigid, stereotyped ideas about sex roles and intimacy, and their misinformation about sexuality.
5. Providing various skill-training elements, including assertiveness and anger management, to remediate deficits that impede successful functioning.

These five goals have helped us structure our treatment interventions and evaluate the offenders' progress in our treatment program.

 Chapter 7

COMMUNITY-BASED TREATMENT

This chapter highlights our approach to working with adolescent sex offenders and provides clinicians with detailed information on how to develop an outpatient treatment program. Our discussion, focusing on group, individual, and family therapy, includes a discussion of the case-managerial role.

Group therapy is our preferred approach to working with adolescent sex offenders. Individual and family therapy serve as adjuncts to the group. Following are our format for treatment (e.g., goals of therapy), detailed information on how to structure sessions, copies of our handouts and treatment modules for sessions, and some useful suggestions for the assessment of group process.

GROUP THERAPY:
RATIONALE AND STRUCTURE

Group treatment is our preferred modality for several reasons. First, it offers a means by which therapy can be offered to greater numbers of sex offenders. Second, this approach capitalizes upon the peer orientation of adolescents. The confrontation and support offered by other sex offenders is often more powerful than interactions with a clinician in individual therapy. Third, inclusion in a peer group addresses the social isolation, shame, secrecy, and communication difficulties that are elements of the abusive lifestyle pattern (Creeden & Sanford, 1984).

We use the descriptor "group leaders" to describe the clinicians who select participants, plan and conduct adolescent sex offender groups, and coordinate the offender's program. It is preferable for the group to have co-leaders, because of the intensity of the issues addressed in therapy and the challenging interpersonal style of adolescent sex offenders. Ideally, a male-female team should co-lead the group. It is beneficial for the adolescents to be given the opportunity to relate to an assertive, competent woman in a position of authority. Our experience has been that these young men have particular difficulty dealing with females. They feel anxious and inadequate in their relationships with women, and may tend to struggle over control issues with the female leader.

The interactions between the two therapists can provide a model of a cooperative, equal relationship. It is important that the group members see each co-leader take charge of group sessions. The male therapist should not function as the senior partner, as group members will be extremely alert to any indications that the woman is deferring to the man. Both leaders should fill supportive, caring, and confrontive roles.

Our approach to treatment includes the use of group discussion, reporting of relevant experiences occurring between sessions, audiovisual media to stimulate discussion and provide information, values clarification, skill training, and homework assignments. Homework tasks are reviewed at subsequent group sessions.

Our program is housed in two outpatient child and youth facilities. The sex offender-specific work (individual, peer group, and family therapy) is offered in one facility; the communication skills, socialization training, and academic assessment and remediation are held in the other agency. The group treatment services we offer to male adolescent sex offenders are specifically designed for offenders classified as naïve experimenter, undersocialized child exploiter, pseudo-socialized child exploiter, or sexual compulsive. Male adolescent sex offenders classified as sexual aggressive, disturbed impulsive, and group-influenced are not included in our treatment group but are offered other sex offender-specific treatment (e.g., family therapy).

Table 1 (pp. 70-71) highlights the criteria for acceptance in and general structure of the group; this description is sent to agencies and/or professionals who make referrals to us. We have continued to modify this form as the group has developed. For example, we did not specify that the offender must speak English until we were referred an offender who met all the criteria on our list except that he was of native origin and could not speak English. We believe that group leaders need to clearly set out the criteria for acceptance into their group and must follow those criteria.

Offenders can be referred to our group from a variety of sources (e.g., court, social services, from within our clinic). We prefer to accept adolescents who have gone through the court process and have a lengthy sentence, but we have taken non-court-ordered offenders into our group. When an offender is referred whom we have not previously assessed, we arrange two to three sessions to meet with the offender and, when possible, his family. We also arrange to meet with the offender's probation or social service worker, correctional staff if he is residing in a custodial facility, and any other professionals involved with him or his family. Our approach to working with adolescent sex offenders not only involves having the offender attend our group; it also involves having the people connected to the offender become active participants in the therapeutic process. Their tasks may range from monitoring the offender to participating in therapeutic endeavors. Therefore we believe that group leaders should take time to carefully select candidates for their group. We have generally had poor results with cases we accepted too quickly.

Our group is open-ended with a continuous intake. As an offender leaves, we take in another. The maximum number allowed in our group is eight. When we started our group we had thought we could manage 10 to 12 offenders per group. We soon realized that adolescent sex offenders are very demanding clients, and eight was the maximum we could handle. We never allow more than one new member to start at a time, and we try to arrange planned termination for long-term members.

The group meets once a week for 2 to 3 hours. The offenders are required to attend every session. They have to arrange with the group leaders if they will be late or have to miss a session.

We inform the offenders that they are responsible for getting themselves to the group. We will not accept excuses (e.g., "My mother couldn't drive me; the bus was late"). We tell offenders that we view tardiness or failure to take responsibility as danger signs. One offender told us he had never taken a bus and had to wait for his father to drive him. Part of the treatment plan for this youth was to reduce his dependence on his father. We gave him a homework assignment to learn the bus system and take the

69

**TABLE 1: DESCRIPTION OF THE AUTHORS'
ADOLESCENT SEX OFFENDER TREATMENT
GROUP SENT TO OTHER REFERRING
AGENCIES OR PROFESSIONALS**

LEADERS: (Insert names of leaders here)

GROUP STRUCTURE

Criteria for Admission. Prior to acceptance in the group, each adolescent must be seen for assessment by the two group leaders. The following are the essential criteria for inclusion in the group:

1. Adolescents must be 14 to 18 years of age.
2. They must have accepted responsibility for their sexual offenses.
3. Court proceedings must be completed.
4. Group attendance must be mandatory, either as part of the court sentence or via enforcement by some alternative external consequence.
5. Adolescents must be sufficiently intelligent and fluent in English to be able to benefit from and contribute to group sessions.

Group Format. The group is *open-ended.* Referrals are accepted continuously. Adolescents exit the group in a planned manner, once having accomplished clearly established treatment goals.

INVOLVEMENT OF THE REFERRAL SOURCE

1. The group leaders will provide written feedback on a monthly basis to the referral source concerning the young person's response to the group.
2. The referral source will be asked to be involved in treatment planning.
3. The group leaders will notify the youth's referral source if he does not attend a group session.
4. The referral source will be expected to support the group leaders by following up on any absences from group.

HOW TO MAKE A REFERRAL

Contact: (Insert name of designated person here to whom agencies can make referrals)

Documentation of the details of the sexual offenses will be required as well as any background information.

PRIMARY OBJECTIVE

The primary objective is to reduce the likelihood that adolescents involved will commit further sexual offenses.

TREATMENT APPROACHES

1. Group members are encouraged to confront their own responsibility for the sexual offenses and to help one another deal honestly with the emotional conflicts aroused by acknowledging that responsibility.

    Strategies:

    - Group discussion
    - Focus upon the impact of abuse upon the victim
    - Emphasis on perspective-taking aimed at developing empathy for the victim

2. The group emphasizes learning socially effective ways of managing various interpersonal situations.

    Strategies:

    - Social skills training via role playing and modeling
    - Problem-solving training
    - Anger management

3. The families of the group members are included in the treatment program whenever possible. This might mean ongoing family therapy, or less intensive liaison. The goals of family involvement are to assist the families in confronting the sexual offense and in dealing with the effects upon all family members. Treatment gains made in group will be bolstered by therapy for the family.

bus to get to the next group meeting. His father called us and tried to convince us his son would get lost. We told him that his son was 15 and could handle the task. Within a few weeks the offender was taking the bus all over the city.

When an offender is deemed acceptable for our group we arrange a time for him to start. All the adolescent sex offenders we have accepted into the group think other members will fit the stereotype image of offenders outlined in our myth section (Chapter 2, pp. 6-10). The first session always comes as a surprise to them: "They look like me." The stereotyped image fits the offender's style of coping: "I'm the exception to the rule and thus am not as bad as other offenders." The first meeting shatters this belief and forces the offender to reassess himself.

When a new member joins the group, two standard activities occur: explanation of group rules and a member "go-around" (offenders tell one another their sexual offenses).

TWO EXERCISES FOR THE FIRST SESSION

Group Rules. When a new member starts, we begin the first session with a discussion of our group rules. Old members tell the new member the rules. This is useful for the leaders because we can assess if the older members have remembered those rules and are practicing them.

Our group rules are:

1. What is said in the group stays in the group (confidentiality).
2. If an offender reveals that he has committed some new sexual offense or reports previous offenses for which he was not charged, the group leaders will report him to the appropriate authorities.
3. Offenders must talk about their offenses.
4. When talking about their victims, offenders must use the victims' first names.
5. The following words or phrases may not be used by offenders when describing their offenses: just; I don't know; I forget; he or she asked for it.
6. No vulgar or sexist language is allowed in the group.
7. Group members may not talk when someone else is talking.
8. All group members have to attend and participate in group discussions.

9. They must be on time for group meetings.
10. They have to complete homework assignments.
11. Group members should not be judgmental of others.
12. Offenders have to contact group leaders prior to the group meeting if they are going to be late or miss a session.
13. Offenders are responsible for getting themselves to the group.
14. No eating is allowed in the group.

Professionals to whom we have talked about our rules question us most on the second rule. They ask "How can an offender trust you when he knows that you will report him if he tells you about his actions?" They believe that when the offender hears this rule he will probably keep quiet. We have found the opposite to be true: The offender accepts the rule and will discuss his sexual assaults. We have not had one offender refuse to talk because of this rule. There are three reasons why we have incorporated this rule:

1. *Accountability* - Sexual offenses are illegal and the offender must be held accountable for his actions.
2. *Breaking the Shared Secret* - Offenders need to realize that they cannot reduce internal conflict by just sharing with us. They must realize that their offenses are illegal and morally wrong, and society will hold them accountable. Sharing with us will not elevate the consequences of offending.
3. *Prevention* - We inform offenders that they are responsible for offending. If they re-offend they will be held accountable. This is an important component of the relapse-prevention model they will be taught.

As members introduce the rules, we draw out other members and ask them to comment on the reasons for each rule. The leaders offer clarification if offenders cannot recall a rule or have distorted the purpose of the rule.

Members' "Go-Around." The second exercise we use in the first session is what we have termed "the go-around." In this exercise, each member tells the other members of the group about his offenses. The older members generally go first and the new member last. We inform the new member ahead of time that he will be required to tell the group about his offenses. Key rules the offenders have to follow when telling their story are:

1. No minimizing (e.g., "I only did this").
2. No rationalizing (e.g., "She seduced me").
3. No denial (e.g., "I forget what happened").
4. Victims' first names must be used.
5. Offense patterns must be gone through in detail.
6. Responsibility for their offenses must be taken. (We have the offenders use "I" statements when describing their actions, e.g., "I touched her between the legs.")
7. No sexist language.
8. Eye contact must be made with other members when telling their story.

The group leaders need to monitor the older members when they are discussing their offenses. This gives leaders the opportunity to observe if the offenders are taking responsibility for actions, showing any genuine signs of remorse for the victim, and showing understanding of why they committed offenses. We have found that some members claim they have changed, but when asked to describe what they did, they fall back into old habits (e.g., minimizing, denying, etc.). These exercises can be used throughout the therapy process.

Some programs require the members to review their offenses at the beginning of each session. We have found this procedure time-consuming; also, it allows offenders to start rehearsing what they are going to say. However, we have found that the therapeutic process of each session usually requires at least one member to discuss his sexual offenses. In cases where new members do not join the group regularly, we suggest planning a monthly "go-around."

FOUR-WEEK CYCLE FOR GROUPS

The structure of our group revolves around 4-week cycles. We initially had no structure and operated the group on a traditional group psychotherapy model (i.e., deal with issues as they arose; if no one wants to talk, select someone). This procedure had some benefits (e.g., offenders couldn't predict who would have to talk), but we found that it made it difficult to monitor the offenders' progress, plan structured activities that take more than one session, and deal with skill deficiencies. The unstructured format also did not place enough of the responsibility on the offender for being actively engaged in planning and working on his own issues.

The 4-week cycle came about as a way for us to (a) plan activities that would take more than one session (e.g., feeling identification and expression exercises); (b) have a summary session at the end of each month; (c) plan for termination of old members and admission of new members; and (d) assess group process. At the end of each 4-week cycle, we met to discuss the progress of the group and of the group members.

The last week of each month we arrange to meet with each offender individually, to assess his progress in the group and plan personalized objectives for the next month. These objectives involve both sex offense-related tasks (e.g., talk more openly about offenses in group) and general behavioral or cognitive changes (e.g., join a club). After meeting with all the members we consider what direction the group should move in the next month. For example, should we focus on emotions, taking responsibility, relapse prevention, sex education, and so on, and how will we do it?

Every topic we discuss in our group is linked back to the offenders' offense pattern. Drawing such connections requires that group leaders have good psychotherapy group skills; detailed knowledge about adolescent sex offenders' development and functioning; an understanding of how this knowledge of offenders applies to each member of the group; and a conceptual plan for each offender in the group.

It is difficult to provide specific, step-by-step procedures group leaders can use with adolescent sex offenders, because the content will vary with the types of offenders in each group. Some of our prearranged strategies worked exceptionally well with one set of offenders, while with other offenders they were not useful. We have worked with some clinicians who look for a standard package of techniques they can follow. These clinicians generally are experienced with skill-development groups (e.g., assertiveness skill training) for which such standardized procedures are appropriate. Adolescent sex offenders need skill training, but it is only one component of a complex set of treatment approaches.

The central component of therapy with adolescent sex offenders involves the alteration of deviant thought and behavior patterns. We believe the only method of achieving these objectives is long-term adolescent sex offender-specific treatment. It is generally accepted in the field that a sex offender requires at least 2 years of intensive treatment (National Task Force, 1988).

Examples of Potential Techniques

Group Secretary. The experience of assuming responsibility for recording group topics and homework assignments for each member enhances the offender's sense of involvement and encourages group members to hold one another accountable. A secretary record form includes the date, secretary name, attendance, issues covered in group, homework assignments, concerns, and general comments.

Journal. The journal is intended to assess sexual fantasy life. Group members are to record at least one fantasy daily and bring their journal to group. The leaders read the journals weekly.

Sexual Issues and Education. Adolescent sex offenders need a great deal of education about human sexuality (facts, feelings, and their interaction). The offenders also have to explore their own sexual development, values, misperceptions, experiences, feelings related to sexuality, and fantasies. Salter (1988) has provided some useful exercises. Table 2 (p. 77) provides an example of an exercise we modified (a "sexual autobiography") which explores the offender's sexual thoughts, experiences, feelings, and fantasies. The offenders complete the form as a homework exercise, and we spend a number of group sessions discussing their responses.

Values-Clarification Exercises. These moral-reasoning tasks serve as tools for both assessment and treatment. They allow the leaders to gather information about the offender's personal values concerning sexuality and relationships, and to examine those beliefs interactively as alternative points of view are presented. We have focused on male and female sex-role issues because we see a direct connection between distorted values in that area and the use of power to obtain sex. A sample values-clarification exercise is the "Alligator River Exercise" discussed previously.

**TABLE 2: SEXUAL AUTOBIOGRAPHY OF ADOLESCENT
SEX OFFENDERS USED IN OUR GROUP***

The purpose of this exercise is to have offenders discuss their sexual history, experiences, abuse, feelings, fantasies, and attitudes. We have found this structured exercise useful in having the offenders provide us with information about their past which we can use to help them change. For example, one offender reported never having been sexually abused, but as we went through the exercise, he developed a greater understanding of sexual abuse and reported abuse by an uncle.

QUESTIONS/DISCUSSION

1. Early sexual memories and experiences. How did the offender learn (e.g., modeling, education, humor, and myths) about sex? Explore the influence of the family, peers, teachers, church community, and pornography.
2. Offenders' victimization - emotional, physical, and sexual abuse.
3. Masturbation: Explore onset, frequency, antecedents, fantasy content, and offender's perceptions about masturbating (e.g., "Does he perceive it as natural or perverted?").
4. Use of pornography: What type? When does he use it? Why does he use it? What are his feeling about the content?
5. Dating experiences: Begin with initial experiences (e.g., kissing, petting) and progress to a detailed discussion of sexual experiences (intercourse). Need to explore for both heterosexual and homosexual experiences.
6. General sexual information: How does the offender select partners? What are his reasons for engaging in dating and consensual sexual contact? How does he feel about his sexual experiences?
7. Within the context of items 5 and 6, explore how the offender establishes relationships. How does he select partners? How does he communicate his desires to them?
8. Clinicians also need to explore the offender's fantasies about dating and consensual sex activities.

---

*We have modified this exercise from one developed by Salter (1988).

Video Exercises. We use videotapes concerning a variety of relevant topics to stimulate discussion and to teach. There exist many useful videos dealing with victimization (e.g., *"To a Safer Place"**) and sexuality that we have used productively. We have also videotaped a variety of in-group exercises, including role playing an offender's apologies to victims and other family members.

Feeling Exercise. Offenders as a group tend to have a very restricted understanding of emotions. The leaders must begin with exercises such as feeling charades, and only then progress to examination of the feelings associated with various experiences (e.g., offenders' victims' feelings and their own feelings if they were victimized).

Psychoeducational Material. Richardson et al. (1988) have provided a very useful curriculum for the education of adolescent sex offenders and their families. The goal of such programming is to address the misconceptions upon which offenders base their attempts to minimize and rationalize their offenses. The curriculum covers victimization, offending, human sexuality, and group process.

Reenactment of Offenses. We have each offender talk through the events (internal dialogues and feelings) that led up to his offense, and then discuss his feelings and thoughts during the offense. The goal is to work toward a complete understanding of his pattern of offending.

Relapse Prevention. Table 3 (pp. 80-81) provides an overview of our modified approach to Pithers et al.'s (1988) relapse prevention model.

Written Assignments. We make use of written homework assignments to address various topics including sexual history, experiences of powerlessness, impact of abuse experiences, and current frustrating experiences.

"To a Safer Place" is a 58-minute film of how one woman has come to terms with her life as a survivor of incest. Purchase inquiries should be directed to the National Film Board of Canada (telephone: 306-975-5867); or by contacting the National Clearinghouse on Family Violence (telephone: 1-800-267-1291).

Reaching-Out Exercises. Homework assignments also include tasks such as seeking out new recreational activities, reaching out to peers, and breaking old habits of relying upon others to make choices.

Skill Training. Young sex offenders as a rule are lacking in some basic coping skills (e.g., anger management, assertiveness). We refer our group members to such programing at the youth-serving agency for whom one of the leaders works.

Family Issues. A great deal of attention is given in group to family relationships as they have related and continue to relate to the sexual offending behaviors. The topic may be approached through discussion, role playing of important interactions, and viewing videotapes. Information about intrafamilial abuse will sometimes emerge for the first time in group.

Socialization with Age-Appropriate Peers. We discuss in the group how social isolation is a contributing factor in offending, and have the offenders work at establishing both male and female friends.

Future Planning. We help offenders plan for schooling, employment, dating, marriage, and so on.

Group leaders must be able to modify these exercises for their existing group. Our experience indicates that no single exercise will change an offender, but rather a combination of them over a long period of time is necessary. Offenders in our group have usually had repeated exposure to all these exercises. For example, a central component in our termination process is to have the offender who is leaving group work through his relapse prevention plan. As he works on his model, the other group members are required to help him develop his plan but must also be working on their own plan. At one point in our group, we had two members leave within a 4-month period. This allowed the group to have two exposures to the relapse prevention model in a short period of time.

It is important for the group leaders to have a standardized method of recording their interactions with the offenders in their group. We have developed a group summary note to keep a record of our interactions and to speed the paperwork process. The components of our sex-offender group note include the date,

TABLE 3: A MODIFIED VERSION OF THE
RELAPSE PREVENTION MODEL
DEVELOPED BY PITHERS ET AL. (1988)

Relapse Process	Descriptions/Questions

Phase I - Identification of offense patterns and styles of coping prior to being apprehended

Early Antecedents and Specific Determinants	What are the things that happen to you prior to committing your offenses (emotionally, physically, mentally/cognitively, in your environment)?
Apparently Irrelevant Decisions	What choices did you make that led to you committing the offenses?
High-Risk Situation	Describe situations in the past that put you in risk of re-offending.
	What are the situations now that would put you at risk of re-offending?
Inadequate Coping	How did you try to stop yourself from re-offending in the past?
	Why didn't it work?

Phase II - Focus on developing coping strategies that will prevent future offenses

Training	What do you need to change (cognitively, behaviorally, affectively, socially, sexually, within your family, environmentally, developmentally)?
	How will you know you made these changes?
	How will you maintain these changes once you leave the group?

Relapse Process	Descriptions/Questions
	Phase III - The offender has to become aware of the warning signs that indicate he is regressing into an offense pattern
Lapse	You start to fantasize about re-offending
Abstinence Violation Effect	You tune out control procedures
Relapse	You re-offend
	Phase IV - The offender has to develop a long-term relapse-prevention plan. We help the offender develop a plan he can use for the rest of his life

attendance, topics covered, material to be followed up on, summary of session, concerns about individual members, and a miscellaneous section (e.g., letters to send out).

GOALS OF THE GROUP

The five primary goals of our group sessions are:

1. Acceptance of responsibility
2. Development of empathy for their victims
3. Development of a survival strategy
4. Reeducation
5. Development of personal competency

Acceptance of Responsibility. Adolescent sex offenders have a tendency to minimize and lie about their offenses. They can be masters at providing rationalizations for the offenses and externalizing blame. For example, the offender may claim that he had intercourse with a 6-year-old girl because she did not ask him to stop, and he therefore assumed it did not upset her.

Treatment issues that must be addressed in this area are:

- Denial, minimization, and projecting of blame
- Accountability for offending and exploitive behaviors
- Thinking errors, misperceptions, and myths about offending
- Responsibility in admitting to the offenses and in actively planning to avoid re-offending
- Elimination of irresponsible decision making in various areas of functioning (e.g., relationships, school)
- Resolution of power and control issues and finding socially appropriate ways to meet these needs
- Developing awareness of their sense of helplessness and lack of control, and how those feelings have related to sexual offending
- Impulsivity and poor judgment
- Arousal patterns and deviant fantasizing
- Sex-role stereotyping
- Family functioning and sibling issues

Various techniques will help offenders assume responsibility for their offenses and increase their knowledge about the thoughts, feelings, and circumstances that preceded the sexually assaultive behavior. Sexual offending is conceived of as the culmination of a series of decisions made by the offender. We teach offenders to interrupt this decision-making process by identifying the choices they made that served as precursors to their sexual assaults. A useful tool in helping the offender identify this process is to have him report to the group about the details of his offending behaviors and discuss the precursors to specific offenses. The procedure we use is a modification of the relapse prevention model discussed by Pithers et al. (1988).

As leaders, we model supportive challenging of various attempts at denial and rationalization. Gradually other group members take over that role. The completion of written homework between group sessions helps adolescents begin to examine the thoughts and feelings that precede their impulses to offend.

Development of Empathy for Their Victims. The development of empathy for their victims in adolescent sex offenders is facilitated by group discussion. It is enhanced through viewing films of victims describing the crimes committed against them and their emotional responses to those experiences. A particularly powerful approach is to have adult survivors of abuse attend group sessions to describe the immediate and longer term effects of victimization. Offenders are far less able to deny the relevance of victim statements when they find themselves face-to-face with people who express strong emotions concerning abuse and offenders. The other effect of this technique is to pressure offenders to respond to victims' questions regarding their offense patterns (Reid, Orchard, & Sandre, 1991).

Helping offenders develop empathy is both a crucial and a very difficult goal to achieve. Adolescent sex offenders tend to be adept at avoiding painful emotions. To develop empathy, they must cease to externalize blame and must relinquish their pattern of minimizing the significance of their acts. Sex offenders must come in contact with the sorrow, regret, and self-disgust related to their offenses. One approach that enhances the offenders' identification with their victims is requiring them to refer to their victims by first name. This seems to humanize the victims, making it more difficult for offenders to distance themselves (Ross, 1988). For those offenders who have been victimized, this task must also entail recognition of the pain associated with their own earlier experiences. If even one group member is able to work on that issue in the group, other members can develop greater awareness of the impact of their own sexual offenses.

Treatment issues that must be addressed to help the adolescent sex offender develop empathy for his victims are:

- Identification and expression of emotions (e.g., anger, love)
- Development of good listening skills so he can identify others' emotions
- Understanding the negative impact of his abuse on his victims
- Constructing a series of apologies to his victims
- Dealing with his own victimization (sexual or physical abuse)
- Identification of emotions prior to, during, and after offenses
- Comprehension of how anger, stress, and values influence his reactions to others

Development of a Survival Strategy. Once the adolescent sex offender has accepted responsibility for the offending behavior and understands the reasons why his assaults are harmful to his victims, he can begin to work on understanding his offense pattern. The offense pattern refers to the events, thoughts, and feelings that preceded his sexual offenses. He must examine the experiences he underwent prior to the assaultive act by generating answers to the following questions:

- For how long had I been planning the offense?
- What events took place prior to the offense that may have triggered my behavior?
- Was I angry at someone?
- Was I feeling sad or lonely?
- Was I feeling like a failure?
- Was I feeling sexually aroused?
- Had I masturbated to fantasies of sexual aggression?
- How did I choose my victim?
- How did I isolate my victim and gain his or her cooperation?
- How did I make sure the victim would not tell?
- How did I feel during and after the assault?

Responses to these and other questions help the offender begin to (a) understand his offense pattern as a sequence of interacting variables that led him to commit offenses; (b) realize he has to develop a strategy that will stop him from committing future offenses; (c) plan ways to intervene early in the sequence to prevent a repetition of the offending behavior; and (d) identify potential warning signs that indicate he might be at risk of re-offending and must seek help. The offender develops a plan and then shares it with significant people in his life (e.g., parents, girlfriend). The purpose of the sharing is to elicit support and help. Pithers et al. (1988) have termed this sequence of events "relapse prevention."

Treatment issues that must be addressed in therapy to help the offender develop a survival strategy include:

- Seemingly irrelevant decisions that set up the circumstances for offense and can put the offender at risk of offending in the future (e.g., "It's alright for me to go into the bathroom when my sister is bathing")
- Understanding offending behaviors and offense patterns
- Irresponsible decision making that contributed to the risk of offending
- Long-term management of sexually deviant impulses

- Power and control variables that lead to offending
- Impulsivity and poor judgment
- Arousal patterns and deviant fantasizing
- Sex-role stereotyping
- Sexual identity issues (e.g., homosexuality, heterosexuality)
- Family functioning and siblings issues

Reeducation. Just as it is imperative to help the adolescent develop a survival strategy, it is equally important to help him understand the complex issues related to sexuality and intimacy. Most offenders with whom we have worked have subscribed to misconceptions about male sexuality that emphasize power and dominance. The interrelationship of sexual needs and emotional intimacy is not recognized by the offenders.

For many adolescent offenders, the task of labeling their own emotional needs is initially overwhelming. Our treatment approach incorporates values-clarification exercises, introspective homework assignments, educational components, and group discussion. The group members are challenged and supported to generate a greater understanding of their own needs for nurturance, intimacy, and sexual gratification. They are also asked to focus on the means by which they can meet those needs.

Often, particularly in the early stages, unworkable strategies are developed. An initial survival strategy often generated by the youths involves total abstinence from sexual gratification. The adolescents assume they can simply control their sexual desires via denial or suppression. During the process of education and personal discovery, we try to challenge the validity of such coping strategies by broadening the concept of human sexuality beyond genital activities.

Treatment issues that must be addressed to help the offender develop a more healthy lifestyle are:

- Values clarification (e.g., role of men and women)
- Ability to experience pleasure in nonexploitive activities
- Substance abuse or other addictive behaviors that need to be controlled
- Enhancement of self-esteem
- Positive sexual development and identity
- Sex education (e.g., the facts, feelings, and fantasies that arise out of a healthy sexual approach to life)
- Sex-role stereotyping

- Sexual identity
- Family functioning and sibling issues

Development of Personal Competency. The majority of the adolescent sex offenders we have treated tend to lack a sense of themselves as competent individuals. They experience difficulty in relating effectively to peers and adults, and often express anger and frustration in unacceptable ways during such interactions. They appear to benefit from the opportunity to experience a positive relationship with two caring adults. The two group leaders seem to fulfill parental roles by acknowledging the youths' personal strengths and accomplishments while also providing ways for them to understand and deal with their personal problems.

The communication skill deficits of these youths are addressed within group and individual sessions and by referral to adolescent groups specifically addressing areas of deficit (such as assertiveness training and/or anger-management training). Within the group, the approach includes education, role playing, and monitoring the homework practice of various skills.

Treatment issues that arise due to a lack of skills are:

- Communication and social skills training
- Assertiveness training
- Dating and relationship-building skills
- Anger management and frustration training
- Stress identification and management
- Feeling identification, management, and expression
- Employment and vocational issues
- Educational issues

TASKS FOR GROUP LEADERS

ASSESSMENT OF POTENTIAL
CANDIDATES FOR THE GROUP

In order to make decisions about how suitable an offender is for community-based treatment, the interviewer must gather information concerning the risk of re-offending. The offender and parent interview guidelines, risk checklist, and consultation discussed in the chapter on assessment can help the interviewer in making these decisions.

Our Procedure. We have found that it is essential that both group leaders be present to meet with potential group candidates and, when possible, with their families.

We generally have two meetings with the offender and his family. One of these is used as a feedback session. The assessment sessions range from 1 hour to 90 minutes; we hold a planning meeting between the two sessions which varies in length from 30 minutes to 90 minutes. These sessions include the administration of psychometrics.

We attempt to make contact by phone or in person with the offender's child welfare worker and/or his probation worker prior to and after our assessment. Meeting with the worker in person requires more time; the tentative range is 1 to 3 hours.

We then write a report and send it to the appropriate referral source. This process takes approximately 3 hours.

GROUP SESSIONS

Our Procedure. Our group sessions are co-led by a female and a male therapist.

1. The group meets once a week for 2 hours.
2. Because the group makes use of an opened-ended psychoeducational/psychotherapy group approach to treatment, the leaders must spend planning time prior to the group sessions. This planning time varies from 30 minutes to several hours, and will be extended when the participants keep daily journals that must be read weekly by the leaders.
3. After each session the leaders need to meet and debrief. This time, used to discuss the group and concerns about individual members, is essential because it allows the leaders to maintain focus and to arrange meetings for the next week (e.g., a meeting with an offender's family or social or probation worker). Time ranges between 30 and 90 minutes.
4. The leaders also need to allow time to attend a variety of case conferences. A large percentage of offenders will be on probation and/or be wards of social services agencies. These agencies continually monitor the progress of the offender. In addition, a number of other treatment and/or holding agencies will be involved with the offender and his family. For example, one case we worked with

required that we attend monthly meetings along with 10 other professionals/para-professionals. Each meeting lasted about 90 minutes. Therapists should plan on roughly an hour per week for case conferences.

INDIVIDUAL AND FAMILY SESSIONS

Our Procedure. It is impossible to deal with all of the concerns of the offenders in our group sessions. This has led us to arrange individual and family sessions.

Individual sessions focus on helping offenders deal with individual issues related to offending patterns (e.g., setting goals he will work on in the group), nonoffense-related problems (e.g., school problems), and positive aspects of their lives which they do not have time to share in group (e.g., a part-time job). We also use these sessions to provide the offender with feedback on his progress in the group. This process takes roughly 2 hours per week.

The family sessions have two major functions. They allow the group leaders to monitor home environments and to provide family therapy to families of the offenders. This is especially important in cases of incestuous sexual abuse. One of the major goals of intervention is to establish a home environment that will place controls on the offender so he is less likely to re-offend. We have found it useful for the group leaders also to conduct the family therapy sessions. This provides them with relevant home data on the offender, allows them to assess if the offender is practicing the skills he is learning in the group, and provides material to be used in the group (e.g., empathy for victim). The difficulty lies in finding therapists who have both group (psychoeducational and group psychotherapy) and family therapy skills to conduct the groups and family sessions. An additional difficulty we have encountered is finding the time to handle the group and family commitments.

CONSULTATIONS AND EDUCATION

Our Procedure. Over time we found an increasing demand for our services by community agencies, who requested that we attend case consultations and provide training for their staff. We had to balance these demands with our clinical duties.

Case Consultation. The adolescent sex offenders in our group are also involved with a number of other community agencies (e.g., school, foster placements, correctional centers, etc.). These facilities make numerous requests of the group leaders for information and consultation.

Training Other Professionals. Other professionals and paraprofessionals who come in contact with adolescent sex offenders have contacted us to provide training programs. We have handled these requests by presenting papers and conducting workshops.

GROUP LEADERS' TRAINING

Clinicians working with adolescent sex offenders need the time to continue their own development. This time could be used to review literature, consult with other adolescent sex offender providers, plan research projects, and so forth.

Our Procedure. We schedule time each week to focus on our own training. This time is as important as clinical time with clients because it helps us focus on new ideas and approaches to helping our clients. We have also found this to be a valuable way of retaining our energy and forestalling burnout.

EVALUATION OF ADOLESCENT SEX OFFENDERS IN THE GROUP

In planning a group treatment intervention for adolescent sex offenders, clinicians must also develop some way of evaluating their progress in the group. Attendance in the group alone is not a sign that the offender has changed. Group leaders must continually monitor the offenders' progress on all the issues highlighted under each of the treatment goals. Any signs of not participating should be reported to the probation officer. We have found the probation order to be a strong external motivator for the offender. We take any violation of the treatment agreement (e.g., not completing homework assignments, tardiness, refusal to talk in group) as a sign of failure to comply with treatment which must be reported.

Our involvement in monitoring the offenders' progress in the community provides us with behavioral data to determine if the offender is making genuine changes. Time devoted to attending meetings and conducting family therapy sessions provides group leaders with data on the offenders, which can then be used in group. For example, one offender (who had been removed from the home) reported to the group that everything had gone splendidly on his first weekend visit home. We had talked with the parents who, in contrast, felt the weekend had been disastrous. We used their information to confront the offender in group. He reported that he wanted us to think everything was great - an indication that he needed a great deal more work.

We gauge progress in treatment according to the following criteria:

1. Attendance at all group sessions
2. Participation in group discussion involving self-disclosure, questioning of others, and confrontation of others
3. Completion of homework assignments
4. Verbal messages delivered in the group that demonstrate acceptance of responsibility
5. No evidence of re-offending, including responsible behavior in avoiding risk situations
6. Changes in various skills including anger management, decision making, and social skills
7. Changes in perceptions of male/female relationships and sexuality
8. Changes in community functioning, including adequate school attendance or job performance

This evaluation is based on the group leaders' interactions with and observations of the adolescent sex offender during the course of therapy.

Evaluation of the long-term impact of treatment will require monitoring of community functioning and offending behaviors over time. In our opinion, 5 years might be considered an adequate period for measuring recidivism.

CASE STUDY: KIRK

Kirk was a 16-year-old male who had sexually assaulted two children while babysitting. The incident involved intercourse and oral sex.

The children involved were aged 1 and 3. The incidents went undisclosed for a period of several weeks until the 3-year-old told his mother. When confronted by the police, Kirk confessed to both assaults.

He was taken to Youth Court and sentenced to 2 years probation, yet left in his mother's home. Had we been asked to conduct an assessment of Kirk prior to sentencing we would have recommended that he be placed outside his mother's home. His younger siblings were of comparable ages to his victims. His mother had coopted Kirk to function as her partner and co-parent. She behaved toward him in a highly dependent and often sexualized manner. She was unable to monitor his behavior or to insure the safety of the younger children. She continued to require Kirk to babysit even after the probation worker (and therapists) had ordered her not to.

Kirk had the following indicators of high risk of re-offending:

1. More than one victim
2. Victims of both sexes
3. Complete disregard for his victims' objections
4. A tendency to blame his victims
5. No remorse for the impact on the child victims
6. Numerous social problems
7. School problems (truancy, failing grades)
8. Victim of emotional abuse (suspected sexual abuse)
9. Highly dysfunctional family
10. Family not supportive of treatment

Given the pattern, we would have recommended placement in an open-custody juvenile correctional facility while Kirk received outpatient treatment, with a long-range view to independent living.

COURSE OF TREATMENT

Kirk was ordered to attend our treatment group as a condition of his probation. He presented as superficially compliant, polite, and willing to talk in group. However, we soon became aware of his efforts to share only certain information while continuing to protect family secrets. We observed that Kirk's community behavior was not as innocent as he would have us believe. Information from the school indicated that Kirk had not attended in several weeks and had been expelled. The city police depart-

91

ment informed us that Kirk was suspected of having broken into several homes in the company of several other youths.

We established contact with Kirk's probation officer and arranged a meeting with Kirk and his mother. At that meeting the two received a strong message from the therapists and the probation officer that he was in violation of his probation and could be brought back into court. It was very clear during that meeting that Kirk's continued residence with his mother would impede his progress in treatment. He felt torn between his desire to become independent of her and his fear that she would not be able to cope without him. Clearly, Mrs. K was very fearful of any suggestion that Kirk might move out. Because Kirk was 16 years old, he could not be removed from the home by child welfare. Therefore, the therapy assumed a focus of helping Kirk see how remaining at home was deleterious to him.

The threat of returning to court motivated Kirk to attend therapy and to complete homework assignments. He began to share issues regarding social isolation, feelings of rejection by his father, and a complete absence of self-confidence.

Kirk's mother had been referred to a family therapist but continued to resist treatment. To gauge the safety of the younger children in the home, a welfare parent aide was assigned to visit the home and a babysitter was arranged and paid for by child welfare.

Kirk's progress in treatment has been erratic. He remains far from understanding why he molested the children and continues to alarm us with his lack of empathy. However, he has made some progress in examining his own family history as it relates to his self-consciousness and isolation, and has identified that his ability to play with and manipulate younger children is dangerous. Kirk has yet to examine his relationship with his mother.

Kirk's case illustrates the following important points:

1. A sex offender-specific assessment should be conducted prior to sentencing to inform the judge's decision making.
2. Placement outside the home is essential in cases of severe family dysfunction and sabotaging of treatment.
3. Lengthy probation sentences (at least 2 years) are important to allow sufficient time for change to occur in treatment.
4. Liaising with probation workers and other involved professionals greatly enhances the accuracy of treatment impressions and strengthens the impact of therapy.

INDIVIDUAL TREATMENT

We do not find individual psychotherapy a very constructive approach in helping alter the adolescent sex offender's attitudes or behaviors. However, we do use individual therapy for the following reasons:

1. Individual sessions help orient offenders to the purpose and rules of the group and our expectations of them, and can be a vehicle for developing a therapeutic alliance.
2. Some of the offender's problems are not directly related to inappropriate sexual behaviors and may not be appropriate for group discussion. In other cases, the adolescent may simply need someone with whom to discuss day-to-day problems.
3. We have regular evaluation sessions with each offender in our program. The group leaders provide offenders with descriptions of their progress and help them develop individual goals which they can work on in the group. Some of these goals are related to dealing with inappropriate sexual behaviors while others are related to the individual's personal growth. We have found these planning sessions very useful both for the leaders and the offender.
4. Individual sessions are used for follow-up contacts with youths who have left the program. We are in the process of designing a systematic approach for following up graduates of our program.

We try to arrange for both group leaders to be present during the individual sessions. Their joint presence helps insure continuity.

FAMILY TREATMENT

We attempt to meet with the parents and, if possible, the offender's entire family from the outset of our involvement. There are several purposes for these meetings: (a) to provide the parents with information about our program; (b) to help them understand the need for their support; (c) to express our concerns about possible re-offending (particularly if past victims included family members); (d) to inform them that they (the

93

parents) will be expected to attend a number of family meetings which will be used as a vehicle for sharing information; and (e) to share with them that family therapy may be required. We also use these meetings with the parents to establish a therapeutic alliance with them and to assess their motivation for maintaining their son in our program. Breer (1987) has pointed out that when therapists do not see parents, serious distortions in their perceptions of therapists and the therapeutic process may arise. He states:

> Adolescent offenders frequently minimize the therapeutic content of their treatment. They give the impression to their parents that nothing is really happening. This is sometimes part of a deliberate effort to maneuver their parents into pulling them out of treatment. Parents of offenders have a kind of natural inclination to feel the problem is better brushed under the rug anyway. They need contact with the therapist in order to form some kind of working alliance and to keep their children in treatment. (pp. 139)

Richardson et al. (1988) require that the parents of adolescent sex offenders attend the psychoeducational training program along with the adolescent sex offenders prior to entering the treatment program. They have found that this program provides the parents with information regarding adolescent sex offender development and behaviors, victimization, human sexuality, and the goals of treatment. The training also seems to motivate parents to become involved in the therapeutic process. Our own clinical experience corroborates that of Richardson et al. (1988). We attempt to give the parents as much information about offenders and offense patterns as possible.

In one case a father became hostile toward us, stating that he knew his son better than we could, and asking who we were to tell him about his son. We informed him in a calm manner that yes, he did know his son but that we knew more about adolescent sex offenders, and because his son was an offender, we also had knowledge we could share with him. At this point he asked for more information about offenders, and after receiving the information, became much more cooperative. In another case we responded to a group member's lack of compliance by meeting with him and his mother. The mother had been unsupportive of treatment because her son had been presenting misinformation about the group. Once those issues were clarified her attitude toward us dramatically changed. Subsequently the son's participation in group improved.

One method we have used to provide parents with information about adolescent sex offenders has been to have the parents read Gil's (1987) parental guide to understanding offenders' behavior. It provides the parents with a variety of information in a very readable form. We have used Gil's (1987) publication as a homework assignment for parents and have actually gone through it step-by-step with parents. Sample topics in the guide are: What is a sexual offender? What is known about young sexual offenders? What do we do with our feelings?

Family therapy is not recommended for all the adolescents in our program for a variety of reasons. Some youths do not have intact families. In other cases, when we judge that the offense was the isolated act of a "naïve experimenter," we are likely to deliver sexuality information to both the offender and his parents and focus upon facilitating communication between them. Finally, some parents refuse to attend. We recommend family therapy when (a) the offender and his victims have been residing in the same home (e.g., siblings, stepbrothers, stepsisters, foster children); (b) one or both of the parents have been sexually victimized themselves; (c) the parents are having difficulties parenting and controlling their children, especially the offenders; or (d) families have multiple problems (e.g., children out of control, battering, parents who have been sexually abused).

Not all families are responsive to treatment. Therapists working with adolescent offenders need to work in conjunction with social services in planning for offenders whose family dynamics might contribute to further offending. The recommendation of family therapy in these cases seems to evoke more resistance than individual or group therapy (Breer, 1987). We also use feedback sessions with the offender and parents/families as a means of convincing parents that family therapy would help them cope with issues within the home. We have found that intervening in the home environment is frequently crucial to bringing about and maintaining changes.

Due to our own time constraints, we sometimes refer the families of our group members to other agencies for therapy. Unfortunately this can lead to communication problems and allows the sex offender more opportunity to control the information shared with various treatment workers. The goal of challenging the sex offender's rationalizations and denials is expedited if the same therapists provide group and family therapy. Alternatively, the various elements of the treatment program can be offered by other professionals within the same agency, thereby addressing the issues of consistency of approach and the time constraints of each therapist.

Haley and Madanes (1989) developed a 15-step model for conducting family therapy with adolescent sex offenders. Their approach to therapy is an interactional model that strives for change in the family system. The focus of their model is to reestablish trust and harmony within the family through repentance and acts of restitution by the offender. Haley and Madanes' (1989) model focuses on adolescent incestuous sexual abuse, but can also be used with adolescent sex offenders who commit offenses outside of the family. The steps dealing with victim issues can be modified or ignored and other steps modified to suit each specific case. Haley and Madanes (1989) point out that this model is not appropriate for adolescents who sexually assault other adolescents.

The first 11 steps occur in the first session. The therapist should set aside enough time to complete all 11 steps. Their focus is upon educating the entire family about the impact of sexual abuse, described as a global, spiritual pain affecting all family members. The pain of the victim is particularly emphasized. The offender must state why his offense was morally wrong and illegal, and must apologize to the victim. The apology is not accepted unless judged sincere by all family members, particularly the victim. The victim need not forgive the offender. Next, all other family members apologize to the victim for not having prevented the offenses. The first 11 steps conclude with a discussion of the consequences within the family if the offender re-offends. The consequences must be extremely severe. The victim is helped to choose a protector who is not a nuclear family member. Finally, the offender and family determine means of reparation for the assaults. The reparation must take time to carry out and must have long-term benefits for the victim.

Over the course of ensuing therapy sessions, issues addressed include how the family can help the victim and offender meet their normal developmental needs; how the mother and father can once again love the offender or victim; fostering a healthy sibling relationship between offender and victim; and finally, how the offender can forgive himself so that he can get on with the business of living.

96

The Haley and Madanes (1989) model offers several useful concepts, including (a) the notion of a ritualized apology; (b) the importance of respecting the rights of the victim to withhold forgiveness; (c) the need for all family members to apologize; (d) the emphasis on family-initiated consequences for re-offending, and (e) the ritual of reparation.

Chapter 8

ENHANCING LONG-TERM
EFFECTS OF THERAPY

There appears to be no consistent approach that insures long-term effects of the treatment of adolescent sex offenders. The Stokes and Baer (1977) review of the literature demonstrated that clinicians tend to employ a variety of unsystematic strategies (e.g., train and hope) to insure that clients' therapeutic gains are generalized to their natural environment. They stated that clinicians need to develop a technology of generalization programming. Paquin and Perry (1990) and Perry and Paquin (1987) have provided clinicians with one approach to insuring long-term effects of therapy. They have termed this approach Generalization, Maintenance, and Transfer (GMT).

Generalization refers to efforts to facilitate the spread of skills in the client to behaviors similar to those addressed in therapy but that were not directly targeted. Maintenance refers to persistence over time of the targeted therapy outcome (e.g., offenders stop committing sexual assaults). Transfer refers to efforts to insure that positive changes continue when behaviors targeted in therapy are performed in a new environment or situation.

Paquin and Perry (1990) and Perry and Paquin (1987) believe that strategies for enhancing long-term effects of therapy must be designed prior to initiating treatment programs.

Traditionally, clinicians have assumed that the sole method of insuring durability of treatment gains is to plan follow-up contacts (e.g., booster sessions) once therapy is terminated. Paquin and Perry (1990) and Perry and Paquin (1987) have highlighted that clinicians need to consider treatment durability as a continuous process that starts prior to having the client in therapy, continues throughout the therapeutic process, and systematically plans for posttherapy interventions. They have provided a variety of techniques that can be used during each stage of planning.

The Paquin and Perry (1990) and Perry and Paquin (1987) approach to insuring long-term effects of therapy is applicable to planning therapeutic interventions with adolescent sex offenders. These techniques assist the clinician in organizing his or her interventions with offenders and also focus on enhancing long-term effects of therapeutic interventions.

Perry and Paquin (1987) provided a case example that demonstrated how clinicians could use their GMT techniques to plan an individual treatment intervention with an adolescent sex offender. The techniques were organized under pretherapy, midtherapy, and posttherapy GMT techniques. These strategies could also be used in planning group treatment with adolescent sex offenders.

PRETHERAPY INTERVENTIONS

The focus of the techniques at this stage is to prepare the offender and his family for group treatment intervention.

SELECTION OF OFFENDERS

Therapists should be selective of clients accepted for treatment. All offenders are not suitable for treatment.

CLIENT VARIABLES

Offenders need a strong message from the court that their offenses will not be tolerated by society and that they need to comply with treatment. If offenders fail to do so, they should be returned to the court system where their sentence will be altered (e.g., from probation to open custody placement). This message is a strong motivator to keep offenders attending the group.

THEORETICAL EDUCATION

Richardson et al. (1988) have developed a psychoeducational program that offenders must pass prior to entering treatment.

Offenders attend classes in which they are provided with information on offenders' behavior, victimization, sexuality, and group process. The goal of the curriculum is to provide offenders with knowledge that will help them function in group treatment programs.

FAMILY SUPPORT

Richardson et al. (1988) have the parents of offenders also attend this psychoeducational program. We have used the assessment phase to educate parents about offense behaviors (e.g., Gil, 1987) and elicit their help in monitoring and controlling the offender's behavior, because it is necessary for the family to support the therapeutic process. Often families subtly or actively work to sabotage therapy; in these situations offenders should be removed from home.

CONTRACTS

Ross et al. (1988) have developed a detailed contract that the offender must sign prior to receiving any services from their agency. We have developed our own contract and have used modified versions of Ross et al. (1988). Personalized contracts in conjunction with a court-mandated order to attend therapy are a good combination.

SELF-MONITORING

After the assessment phase and during the educational phase, the therapist may ask adolescent sex offenders to keep a journal of their inappropriate sexual thoughts, conflicts with parents, sexual fantasies, and so on. The focus is to have the offender become aware of his day-to-day functioning.

NATURALISTIC OBSERVATION

Those in charge of the adolescent sex offender (e.g., parents, foster parents, staff in a facility) are asked to monitor specific aspects of his behaviors (e.g., how he handles conflict). The therapist needs outside input on the offender's behaviors due to the offender's tendency to minimize problems.

SKILL TRAINING

Prior to attending our adolescent sex offender group we have had some offenders take some specific skill training programs (e.g., communication skills, assertiveness). The purpose of these interventions is to provide them with skills to function within our treatment group.

MIDTHERAPY INTERVENTIONS

As outlined by Perry and Paquin (1987), the major concern for the therapist during this phase involves coordinating all the therapeutic endeavors. Adolescent sex offenders in our treatment group are usually involved in individual and family therapy; at some point they may be involved in a variety of other structured activities (e.g., recreational, social skills, problem solving, date-initiation skills groups) that need to be coordinated with sex offender-specific treatment. Clinicians can use a variety of strategies. They need to be creative in their endeavors to insure that offenders are altering their sexual offending thoughts and behaviors and are practicing more appropriate ways of meeting their needs. Therapists must be equally creative in coordinating all the agencies involved with the offender to insure a systematic delivery of service. A number of the techniques that we will discuss are currently used in other therapeutic programs. We suggest that clinicians working with adolescent sex offenders carefully plan the strategies they will use with offenders. For example, when assigning tasks such as self-monitoring (e.g., journals), therapists need to set time aside to read each offender's weekly entries, which can become a time-consuming task.

The GMT concept can also be applied to therapeutic intervention with adolescent sex offenders. The first consideration is to insure that offenders acquire the knowledge and skills that will help them eliminate their sexual offending behaviors. The second step is to develop methods of maintaining these acquisitions. The third step is to help the client transfer these new acquisitions to the community. Once offenders have practice transferring knowledge and skills, they can begin practicing generalization.

OPEN REFERRAL POLICY

New members can be added to the group any time, which means that some of the material will have to be reviewed a number of times in the group. The leaders can draw on long-term members to discuss material previously covered, a practice that provides leaders with data on how much information the offenders have processed.

HOMEWORK ASSIGNMENTS AND ASSESSMENT

Throughout the course of therapy, offenders should be given a variety of homework assignments that focus on helping maintain knowledge (e.g., reading material related to offending); transferring specific skills (e.g., role playing how to handle a problem with an offender's father in the group, then having the offender go home and practice it); and generalization (e.g., if an offender has a conflict with his sister, have him review material on how he learned to handle conflicts/problems with his father and then have him apply this knowledge to the problem he is having with his sister).

RELAPSE PREVENTION

We have modified a procedure developed by Pithers et al. (1988). The purpose of this intervention is to help adolescent sex offenders realize that they will be at risk of re-offending for the rest of their lives, and need to develop plans that will help them cope after the termination of treatment. The general components of this procedure are (a) develop a thorough understanding of the factors (both internal and external) that led them to commit their offenses; (b) identify situations in the future that would likely place them at high risk for re-offending; (c) develop ways to cope with these high-risk situations; (d) develop strategies for monitoring and protecting themselves from re-offending after they leave the group; and (d) formulate a contract to specify that should they find themselves relapsing into an offense mode, they will contact a therapist.

SELF-MONITORING

It is useful to have the offender continuously monitor his thoughts, feelings, and behaviors throughout therapy (e.g., keep a journal). The journal provides the therapist and group with relevant information and sometimes indicates how the offender may be changing as a result of his involvement in the group.

PEER PROGRAMMING
AND PEER REINFORCEMENT

The adolescent sex offender process group allows offenders to be confronted by their peers and to receive support from their peers for attempts to change.

ENCOURAGE THE OFFENDERS TO BECOME
INVOLVED IN PLANNING THEIR PROGRAM

We meet with the members of our adolescent sex offender group every 4 weeks to discuss their progress and to plan for the next 4 weeks. The therapists state the issues they consider important but also encourage the offenders to come up with issues upon which they would like to work.

ENCOURAGE GROUP CONTINGENCIES

Group leaders need to stress that the goal of the group is to help all participants stop their offending behaviors. The participants need to feel committed and responsible to each other and should be encouraged to confront and support each other.

FAMILY SUPPORT

It is important to maintain the family's support throughout therapy. In some cases the family/parents have become involved in family therapy with the adolescent. In other cases, although offenders' families have not been involved in therapy, we have arranged regular contact sessions where the group leaders and offenders inform the parents on how the offenders are doing in therapy and receive feedback on how they are doing at home.

POSTTHERAPY INTERVENTIONS

Our approach to working with most adolescent sex offenders includes a long-term involvement. Ideally, we like to have offenders involved in our program over a 2-year period. The actual length of time they are involved in the group varies depending on the individual case. We prefer to have an extensive period of time in which the youth can be released from attending the group and begin functioning on his own.

It is important to have some type of phase-out from the group. Initially we thought of having the offenders begin to attend fewer sessions (e.g., come to every third meeting). This process was disruptive to the group and the offender was no longer in touch with group dynamics. We decided that when the group leaders felt it was appropriate, they would arrange a termination date with the offender and the group would be told. This process has worked very effectively in our group.

Prior to termination from the group, we plan a series of follow-up contacts with the offenders and their families. The purpose of these sessions is to monitor the offender's progress and, when needed, to provide "booster sessions" (e.g., help offenders revamp a component of their relapse prevention strategies). For a number of reasons, we have not always been able to plan these contacts (e.g., the offender moves to another community). The therapist should develop strategies to follow offenders after therapy. For offenders who slip back into old habits, the follow-up sessions help them get refocused. The most difficult aspect of arranging for follow-up contacts is the time it takes to plan sessions and insure offender and family attendance. We are currently considering a variety of alternative procedures to facilitate follow-up (e.g., self-help groups), but have not worked out the details on how to organize these into our treatment strategies.

We have found it less stressful when we inform offenders and their families that therapy involves three phases of treatment: pretherapy intervention, midtherapy intervention, and posttherapy intervention. They are told that each phase is essential to eliminating offending behaviors. In these cases they have been less resistant to the long-term follow-up contacts.

Treatment providers for adolescent sex offenders also need to conceptualize therapeutic intervention with most offenders as a long-term commitment. They need to develop innovative ways of insuring long-term effects of therapy.

 Chapter 9

CONCLUSIONS

Several themes have been highlighted in this book about clinical work with adolescent sex offenders. The foremost goals are to offer clinicians a comprehensive, practical outline of the issues to be addressed in offering treatment services to this population; structuring a group treatment approach; responding to the needs of the families of adolescent sex offenders; and finally, liaising efficiently with other involved professionals and paraprofessionals. Clinicians should be aware of both the rewards and the personally taxing demands of the work. With that recognition will come attention to caring for one's own needs through ongoing training and setting realistic limits. This is a very new treatment area; as such, the clinical literature will continue to increase as various new programs are described. Professionals in the field must be sufficiently versed in theoretical writings on the topic of sexual offending to screen the value of those programs and to select various components for their own use.

Unfortunately, to date the clinical literature has remained descriptive in nature. Few programs report outcome results. Those few that do can offer encouraging findings with recidivist rates as low as 5% (Lafond, 1982). These findings are heartening to those of us working in the field, and certainly lend support to Abel's (1984) contention that early intervention can prevent a chronic pattern of offending behavior. Existing treatment programs must respond to public demands for accountability by collecting long-term (minimum 5 years) follow-up data on the reinvolvement of their participants with the correctional system.

Certainly those data will suffer from inaccuracies associated with depending on police and court statistics. Nevertheless, estimates of recidivism lend credence to statements attesting to the value of treatment programs.

The next stage in the evaluation of treatment programs must be the dissection of the components. This is necessary in order to argue that cognitive therapy elements and/or social skills training bring about valuable change related to reduced recidivism. The usefulness of various treatment components with different groups of offenders (e.g., hands-off offenders versus sexually aggressive offenders) must also be examined. Unless the nature of the sex offenders being served is carefully described, useful treatment approaches may be discarded when they might well be effective with other sex-offender groups. As yet we are unable to use research data to guide the structuring of treatment components. As in many other areas of clinical work, we begin by relying upon practical experience in the field and go on to examine the validity of those clinical judgments.

As we have argued throughout this book, the stakes are high in working with adolescent sex offenders. Ineffective treatment of this population can contribute to increased numbers of abuse victims. In this field, perhaps more than any other, research and therapy must progress in unison.

APPENDICES

SAMPLE GUIDE
FOR INTERVIEWING OFFENDERS

These questions are designed to gather information important in assessing adolescent sex offenders. It is essential to have detailed information about the offender, his offenses, and his family. Each question may be subdivided into a number of related questions, tailored to the particular situation.

Prior to asking any questions, we begin the session with a general lead-in such as:

We are both psychologists, and have been requested to interview you about your sexual offenses. Our job is to make some assessments about your situation, and then to make recommendations to the individuals who referred you. It is not our role to establish guilt or innocence. You have already pled guilty to these charges, and we have information about your charges from the agencies involved. The information you share with us will not be held in confidence. It will be included in our report, which will be sent to the referral source. It is in your best interest to be honest with us. We have the factual data from other sources, but are interested in finding out about these charges from your perspective. Do you have any questions?

We answer all of the individual's questions and then start the interview. We usually interview the offender as a team and take turns asking questions.

QUESTIONS RELATED TO OFFENSES,
VICTIMIZATION, AND SEXUALITY

OFFENSES

We start by discussing the offender's charges.

1. Describe your sexual offending behaviors (the assessor needs to probe for not only the offenses of record, but also offenses for which the youth has not been charged).
2. What exactly did you do to your victims during each of your sexual offenses?
3. Confront discrepancies between the offender's statements and the victim's reports (the assessor must ask very specific questions; for example, "Did you have her touch your penis with hands or mouth?").
4. A specific description is obtained about what the offender recalls feeling, thinking, and doing prior to, during, and after the sexual offenses. We usually do a general overview, then get specifics. Some questions that may elicit this information are:

    a. How were you feeling prior to, during, and after the offenses (e.g., "Were you aroused, angry, sad, etc.?")?
    b. What were you thinking about prior to, during, and after the offenses?
    c. What made you choose this victim or these victims?
    d. How did you set up the circumstances in which to offend?
    e. What did you say to yourself to try to convince yourself that you would not offend?
    f. Once you decided to commit the offense, what excuses did you create for your behavior?
    g. What sexual acts did you think of doing to your victim prior to your offenses?
    h. Why didn't you act on all of those thoughts? *or* What made you do more?
    i. *Nonviolent Offenders* - Did you think of hurting your victims? What prevented you from acting on these thoughts (explore aggressive fantasy life)?
    j. *Violent Offenders* - Did you think of killing your victim? What stopped you from acting on these thoughts (explore aggressive fantasy life)?
    k. What did you get out of your sexual offense?
    l. Were you aroused before you were involved with the victim, or did you get an erection during the offense?
    m. Did you have an orgasm during the assault or after?
    n. What did you do after the offense?
    o. What did you say to yourself after the offense?
    p. How did you feel immediately after; the next day; when you were caught?
    q. What was the payoff for your inappropriate sexual behaviors?
    r. How do you think the victim felt during the offense? What did he or she do or say to make you think he or she felt that way?
    s. What did you say or do to the victim after the offense?

t. How did you convince the victim not to tell? Sometimes a person might say, "Don't tell anyone," or "If you tell, you'll be sorry." What did you say?
u. Did you do anything to prevent future offenses?
v. What other sexual assaults have you committed?
w. What did you think contributed to your re-offending?
x. How did your family members respond to your charges (get specific information about each parent and sibling)?

5. What do you think upsets other people about what you did?
6. What do you think makes what you did wrong or bad?

VICTIMIZATION

7. Has anyone in your family or outside your family ever touched you in a way that made you feel uncomfortable? (It may be necessary to ask specific questions about where the youth was touched.)
8. Has anyone ever hit you when you did something wrong or even when you hadn't? Who? What happened?

SEXUALITY

9. How did you find out about sex?
10. How old were you when you first started to masturbate, and how often do you now masturbate?
11. What was your first sexual experience?
12. Tell me about your sexual fantasies. (The interviewer needs to guide the offender through this process. For example, use material about fantasies to further explore the sexual offenses. If a youth admits to having intercourse with a child but says he masturbates exclusively to fantasies about women his age or older, say, "I'm confused; you're telling me you masturbate to fantasies about older women and yet you choose children to have sex with." Continue to explore his responses.)
13. What do you fantasize about when you are masturbating or are sexually aroused?
14. How do you feel about masturbating?
15. Tell me about your other sexual experiences. (Some authors have a specific list of both consensual and nonconsensual sexual activities - see Coleman, 1988.)
16. What do you do when you are aroused?
17. How do you plan to meet your future sexual needs?
18. What do you plan to do to stop offending?

Note: The interviewer must be sensitive to the need to assess for alternative sexual orientations.

QUESTIONS RELATED
TO SOCIAL RELATIONSHIPS

1. What do you do for fun?
2. Who is your best friend? What makes him or her your best friend?
3. Do you hang around with a group of kids?
4. What things do you do with him/her/them?
5. How often do you get together?
6. Who usually decides to get together?
7. How old are your friends?
8. How do you get along with girls?
9. How do you get along with younger children?
10. How do your parents feel about your friends?
11. Is it all right with your parents for you to bring your friends around the house?
12. Do you ever get into fights? How does that happen? How often?
13. How do you express your anger?
14. Do other young people tease you?
15. How do you get along with youths your age?

GENERAL QUESTIONS

1. Have you ever been in trouble with the police for any other delinquent acts? (Delinquency history)
2. Describe your use of alcohol, illegal drugs, or other substances. (Ask pointed questions about consumption, frequency)
3. Describe your school performance in the last 2 years. How are your marks? Relationship with teachers? Any school-related problems?
4. How do you get along with your parents? (Explore each parent, stepparents, boyfriend/girlfriend of parents, etc.)
5. Whom are you closest to in the family?
6. Who does the disciplining in your family?
7. What kind of discipline is used?

Appendix B

SAMPLE INTERVIEW GUIDE
FOR PARENTS OF OFFENDERS

We generally interview parents as a couple, but sometimes we also interview them separately. The clinician needs to determine if one parent is controlling the discussion. If this happens, one of the parents can be asked to complete an evaluation form (e.g., Family Assessment Measure) while the other one is talked with privately. When the parent has completed the forms or tests, the roles are exchanged. This procedure allows access to the perspectives of both parents regarding the offender. The questions are designed to gather general information on the family and specific information on the offender.

GENERAL INFORMATION
ABOUT PARENTS AND FAMILY

The examiner usually asks a variety of questions to obtain some general information about the family and to establish rapport.

1. How long have you lived at your current address?
2. How many children do you have and what are their names? (Note: These questions can generate a number of alternative questions.)
3. What are your occupations? (Note: From this, assess education and economic adjustment of both parents.)

PARENTAL DESCRIPTIONS
OF THE SEXUAL OFFENSES

1. Please describe in your own words the sexual offenses for which your son has been charged. (Here the assessor should be alert to parental tendencies to deny their son's guilt, minimize the significance of the offenses, or to blame the victim. Any differences in the attitudes of the two parents should also be noted.)

2. What was your response when you found out about the offenses? What was your reaction to your son? Whom have you told about the offenses (e.g., nuclear and extended family members, friends, potential victims)?
3. How have the charges against your son affected you? (Ask each parent.)
4. How has your family been affected? How have they responded to (the offender)? In cases of intrafamilial abuse, be sure to ask how family members have responded to the victim.
5. How do you feel about your son since learning of his sexual offenses?
6. What effects have the offenses had upon his victims?
7. What controls have you placed on your son so that he will not re-offend?
8. Can you think of any warning signs that indicated your son would be capable of the sexual offense? Are there any incidents which you now look back on as early warning signs?
9. Are you willing to participate in your son's treatment as a couple and as a family?
10. How do you think you can help your son deal with these charges and learn not to re-offend?

GENERAL INFORMATION ABOUT THE OFFENDER'S OVERALL LEVEL OF FUNCTIONING

The questions in this section are designed to get specific facts about the offender from the parents' perspective. The clinician can compare the offender's parents' responses to similar questions.

1. Tell me about your son (offender).
2. How does he get along with other family members?
3. How does he feel about school? What are his marks? How does he get along with teachers?
4. Tell me about your son's friends (male and female). Does he have a best friend? How long does he hang onto friends? What are his friends like? How does he get along with girls? Has he ever had a girlfriend? (Explore)
5. How did your son find out about sex?
6. What activities does your son enjoy engaging in (sports, clubs, hobbies, exercise, etc.)? (Note and explore)
7. Has your son ever had a paying job?
8. Has he ever done volunteer work?
9. Has he ever gotten into trouble with the neighbors?
10. Has he ever been in trouble with the law/courts/police prior to his current offenses? If so, what did he do? How did you deal with it?

11. How does (the offender) get along with his brothers and/or sisters?
12. Does he ever bully/boss around his siblings? If so, how does he do so and how do you deal with it?
13. Has he been bullied by his siblings? If so, how has he coped and what approach have you taken to this problem?
14. Who is he closest to in the family?
15. Who is he least close to?
16. How can you cheer (the offender) up when he is sad or discouraged?

CO-PARENTING ABILITIES/MARITAL RELATIONSHIP

1. What approach do you take to discipline in your family?
2. Who tends to enforce the rules most often?
3. What do you do if you disagree about discipline?
4. Whom does (the offender) listen to most?
5. What sorts of activities does your family engage in together (e.g., church, clubs, sports, etc.)?
6. Does (the offender) join in on those activities?
7. What regular quiet times do you have together as a family (e.g., meals, pre-bed routines, homework time)?
8. What times do you spend together as a couple away from your children? What interests do you share?

HISTORY OF SEXUAL, PHYSICAL, OR SUBSTANCE ABUSE

1. To your knowledge, has (the offender) ever been touched inappropriately or ever been made to carry out sexual acts by another person (e.g., by a family member, a babysitter)?
2. Have you, or anyone else in your immediate family, experienced sexual abuse? If the parents acknowledge past abuse, ask what the family reaction was.
3. When the abuse was discovered, what did you do? Or, in instances of abuse in the parent's family of origin: What did the responsible adults do?
4. Did the victims receive support and treatment?
5. Was the offender charged? Treated?
6. Have you been a victim of sexual and/or physical abuse?

PHYSICAL ABUSE

The presence of physical abuse within the nuclear family can be assessed by attending to the responses of the parents to questions regarding disciplinary methods. At times, the assessor may suspect that

117

one of the parents is abusive and that the other is reluctant to speak out. At these times, interviewing the two separately is crucial.

SUBSTANCE ABUSE

Although the assessor may not receive honest answers to direct questioning about substance abuse, various pieces of relevant information can be gathered from parental responses to preceding sections, as well as information available from the referral source. Often, families of alcoholics or drug addicts are known to child welfare officials. In addition, the social life of the parents, the ways in which they handle conflict, and the success of their working life will be influenced by substance abuse.

RISK CHECKLIST FOR OFFENDERS

One of the major responsibilities of the person conducting an assessment of a sexual offender is to consider the potential risk for re-offending. The form provided herein is a modification of the risk factors described by Bengis (1986), Dreiblatt (1982), Jackson (1984), and Perry and Orchard (1989). Sixty-two statements have been arranged into 31 pairs that distinguish *High-Risk Characteristics* from *Low-Risk Characteristics*. The clinician places a check in the appropriate space for each pair. Conclusions may be based on an integration of all of the data collected. After completing this checklist, the clinician can make a decision based on information summarized therein. This is an informal checklist designed to guide interview inquiry. There are no normative data.

Low-Risk Characteristics			High-Risk Characteristics
1. One victim	_____	_____	Numerous assaults on one victim or has had a number of victims
2. No violence	_____	_____	Used physical force, weapon, or threat of violence
3. No compulsive ideation about offenses	_____	_____	Compulsive ideation about offenses (e.g., sexual fantasies revolve around offenses)
4. Terminated assault when victim protested or showed distress	_____	_____	Disregard for victim's objections

Low-Risk Characteristics			**High-Risk Characteristics**
5. Narrow offense range (e.g., only committed one type of assault	_____	_____	A broad range of offending
6. First apprehension for offending	_____	_____	A number of apprehensions for sexual-related charges
7. No escalation in offense patterns	_____	_____	Escalation in offending (e.g., frequency)
8. Sexual offending stopped after contact with the law	_____	_____	Continued to offend after contact with the law
9. No previous treatment for sexual offending	_____	_____	Has received sex offender-specific treatment
10. Admits he committed offenses	_____	_____	Denies he committed offenses
11. Accepts responsibility for planning and carrying out assaults	_____	_____	Blames the victim
12. Has some empathy for victim	_____	_____	Limited remorse for his victim and never considered how assaults were affecting the victim
13. Comprehended the reasons why sexual assaults are morally and legally wrong	_____	_____	Does not understand why assaults are wrong

Low-Risk Characteristics			High-Risk Characteristics
14. Willing to discuss the assaults	_____	_____	Resistant to sharing information; attempts to conceal facts from examiner
15. Has some perceptions on how to prevent future offenses	_____	_____	Limited awareness of how to prevent future assaults
16. Understands he will need help to change	_____	_____	Resistant to becoming involved in treatment
17. Has a flexible belief system with regard to intimacy and sexuality	_____	_____	Rigid belief system with regard to intimacy and sexuality
18. No history of problems; not physically aggressive	_____	_____	History of being physically aggressive
19. No chemical abuse problems	_____	_____	Has a record of chemical abuse
20. Has not been a victim of sexual, physical, or emotional abuse	_____	_____	Victim of sexual, physical, or emotional abuse
21. No history of fire setting or cruelty to animals	_____	_____	History of fire setting or cruelty to animals
22. No substantial delinquent history	_____	_____	History of delinquent behaviors
23. Some awareness of the need to identify and express emotions	_____	_____	Attempts to deal with emotions by suppressing them

121

	Low-Risk Characteristics			High-Risk Characteristics

24. Reasonable social skills   _____   _____   Limited social skills (e.g., assertive skills)

25. Suffering from no other significant emotional, psychological, or behavioral problems   _____   _____   Sexual offending is confounded by some other psychological problem (e.g., psychosis)

26. Cooperative during assessment process   _____   _____   Resistant to the assessment process

27. Has a number of social support networks in the community (e.g., peers)   _____   _____   Offender is a loner with few social supports

28. Parents acknowledge their son's inappropriate behavior and hold him responsible for offending   _____   _____   Parents are highly defensive and unwilling to accept facts

29. Family reasonably functional   _____   _____   Dysfunctional or multiproblem family

30. Family supportive of helping process and willing to participate in treatment   _____   _____   Family not supportive of treatment and unwilling to participate

31. No history of sexual, physical, or emotional abuse of parents or other siblings   _____   _____   History of sexual, physical, or emotional abuse of any family member

Appendix D

RISK FACTOR CONSTELLATION

Risk factors affecting placement and treatment options for adolescent sex offenders are described below.

TREATMENT RECOMMENDATIONS

CLOSED CUSTODY

Closed Custody/No Treatment

1. Offender completely denies having committed the offenses.
2. Offender admits to the offenses but refuses treatment.

Closed Custody with In-House Treatment

1. Offender admits to the offenses and wants treatment but:

   a. is very aggressive;
   b. has a long history of repeated offending against multiple victims;
   c. shows a total disregard for the victim's objections during the offenses;
   d. shows a broad range of sexual misconduct;
   e. is evidencing an escalation in the frequency and/or type of offending;
   f. has experienced prior unsuccessful treatment for sexual offending;
   g. has a history of sexual victimization;
   h. has a history of delinquency;
   i. has engaged in fire setting and/or cruelty to animals;
   j. has many personal problems (e.g., school failures, social limitations);
   k. doesn't understand why the sexual offenses were wrong;
   l. tends to blame his victims;

m.   parents are unwilling to accept the facts and are not supportive of assessment or treatment; and/or

n.   the family has multiple problems.

OPEN CUSTODY CORRECTIONAL PLACEMENT/WITH TREATMENT

Placement in Community Open Custody Home/Outpatient Treatment

1.   The offender admits to his offenses and is accepting of treatment but:

a.   has offended numerous times;

b.   has offended against more than one victim;

c.   has offended against a victim in the home;

d.   comes from a family with multiple problems;

e.   reveals a history of sexual abuse himself by a family member;

f.   tends to blame his victims;

g.   is not able to appreciate the impact he has had upon the victims;

h.   has a history of other delinquent acts;

i.   has a history of substance abuse;

j.   family is not willing to take part in treatment; and/or

k.   family is not likely to be able to enforce restrictions on the offender's behavior.

Open Custody Institution/In-House Treatment

1.   These offenders admit to their offenses and accept treatment.

2.   They reveal all of the maladaptive attributes described in the preceding category and *in addition*:

a.   evidence very limited impulse control and/or

b.   have extremely poor social skills such that they are unlikely to benefit from outpatient treatment, instead requiring intensive daily in-house treatment.

PROBATION DISPOSITIONS

Placement in Foster or Group Homes/Outpatient Treatment

1.   These offenders admit to their offenses and accept treatment.

2.   Major factors that dictate placement outside the home are:

a. the family is unsupportive of treatment;
b. the victims are nuclear family members;
c. there has been physical or sexual abuse within the home; and/or
d. there is current substance abuse within the home.

3. In addition, these offenders:

a. have offended against only one victim;
b. have not used aggression in their sexual offenses;
c. show a narrow range of sexual misconduct;
d. have been apprehended for the first time;
e. evidence no escalation in sexual offending;
f. have had no previous treatment for sexual offending;
g. have less well established patterns of delinquent behavior;
h. show some school dysfunction but at least are still enrolled;
i. have some social relationships, although these may be dysfunctional;
j. have some understanding of why their sexual offenses were wrong;
k. can discuss their offenses;
l. do not blame the victims;
m. have some appreciation of the negative impact on their victims; and/or
n. cooperate with the assessment.

**Placement with the
Biological Family/Outpatient Treatment**

These offenders admit to their offenses, accept treatment, and evidence a pattern of behavior and functioning similar to those offenders who would be recommended to group or foster home placement. However, these offenders have offended against nonfamily members. Another category of distinctions between the two groups is that the families of offenders who can live at home have parents who do not minimize the significance of the sexual offenses, are willing to take part in treatment, show no history of physical or sexual abuse and no ongoing substance abuse, and are judged to be capable of enforcing various restrictions on the offender's behavior as dictated by treatment.

REFERENCES

Abel, G. G. (1984). *The Outcome of Assessment Treatment at the Sexual Behavior Clinic and Its Relevance to the Need for Treatment Programs for Adolescent Sex Offenders in New York State.* Paper presented at a Prison Research/Education/Action Project, Albany, NY.

Anchor, K. N. (1984). Testifying as an expert witness. In P. A. Keller & L. G. Ritt (Eds.), *Innovations in Clinical Practice: A Source Book* (Vol. 3, pp. 367-378). Sarasota, FL: Professional Resource Exchange.

Araji, S., & Finkelhor, D. (1985). Explanations of pedophilia: Review of empirical research. *Bulletin of American Academic Psychiatry Law, 13,* 17-37.

Bengis, S. M. (1986). *A Comprehensive Service Delivery System with a Continuum of Care for Adolescent Sexual Offenders.* Orwell, VT: Safer Society Press.

Bengis, S. M. (1988). Personal/interpersonal issues. In *Proceedings of the Training Intensive for the Treatment of Adolescent Sex Offenders Workshop May/88, Toronto, Ontario* (pp. 82-92). Ottawa, Ontario, Canada: Canadian Child Welfare Association.

Bengis, S. M., & Cunninggim, P. (1989, April). *Working with the Juvenile Offender in Residential and Educational Settings.* Paper presented at Advanced Training for Treatment of Adolescent Sex Offenders, sponsored by Canadian Child Welfare Association, Toronto, Ontario, Canada.

Bera, W. H. (1985). *A Preliminary Investigation of a Typology of Adolescent Sex Offenders and Their Family Systems.* Unpublished master's thesis, University of Minnesota, Minneapolis, MN.

Bera, W. H. (1989, April). *Adolescent Sex Offenders and Their Family Systems.* Paper presented at Advanced Training for Treatment of Adolescent Sex Offenders, sponsored by Canadian Child Welfare Association, Toronto, Ontario, Canada.

Blau, T. H. (1984). *The Psychologist as Expert Witness.* New York: John Wiley & Sons.

Breer, W. (1987). *The Adolescent Molester.* Springfield, IL: Charles C. Thomas.

Burchard, J. D., & Burchard, S. N. (Eds.). (1987). *Prevention of Delinquent Behavior.* Newbury Park, CA: Sage.

Byrne, K. (1985). Conducting the initial forensic interview. In P. A. Keller & L. G. Ritt (Eds.), *Innovations in Clinical Practice: A Source Book* (Vol. 4, pp. 467-474). Sarasota, FL: Professional Resource Exchange.

Coleman, E. (1988). Behavioral assessment and treatment. In *Proceedings of the Training Intensive for the Treatment of Adolescent Sex Offenders Workshop May/88, Toronto, Ontario* (pp. 9-41). Ottawa, Ontario, Canada: Canadian Child Welfare Association.

Corder, B. F. (1987). Planning and leading adolescent therapy groups. In P. A. Keller & S. R. Heyman (Eds.), *Innovations in Clinical Practice: A Source Book* (Vol. 6, pp. 177-196). Sarasota, FL: Professional Resource Exchange.

Cormier, W. H., & Cormier, L. S. (1985). *Interviewing Strategies for Helpers: Fundamental Skills and Cognitive Behavioral Interventions.* Monterey, CA: Brooks/Cole.

Creeden, K., & Sanford, L. (1984). *The Treatment of Juvenile Sex Offenders. A Preliminary Program Description.* Unpublished manuscript.

Davis, G. E., & Leitenberg, H. (1987). Adolescent sex offender. *Psychological Bulletin, 101,* 417-427.

Deisher, R. W., Wenet, G., Paperny, D., Clark, T., & Fehrenback, P. (1982). Adolescent sexual offense behavior: The role of the physician. *Journal of Adolescent Health Care, 2,* 279-286.

Dreiblatt, I. S. (1982, May). *Issues in the Evaluation of the Sex Offender.* A presentation at the Washington State Psychological Association Meeting, Pacific Psychological Services, Seattle, WA.

Egan, G. (1990). *The Skilled Helper: A Systematic Approach to Effective Helping.* Pacific Grove, CA: Brooks/Cole.

Enfield, R. (1987). A model for developing the written forensic report. In P. A. Keller & S. R. Heyman (Eds.), *Innovations in Clinical Practice: A Source Book* (Vol. 6, pp. 379-394). Sarasota, FL: Professional Resource Exchange.

Evans, D. R., Hearn, M. T., Uhlemann, M. R., & Ivey, A. E. (1984). *Essential Interviewing: A Programmer Approach to Effective Communication*. Pacific Grove, CA: Brooks/Cole.

Fersch, Jr., E. A. (1980). Ethical issues for psychologists in court settings. In J. Monahan (Ed.), *Who Is the Client? The Ethics of Psychological Intervention in the Criminal Justice System* (pp. 43-62). Washington, DC: American Psychiatric Association.

Finckenauer, J. O. (1984). *Juvenile Delinquency and Corrections: The Gap Between Theory and Practice*. New York: Academic Press.

Frances, A., Clarkin, J., & Perry, S. (1984). *Differential Therapeutics in Psychiatry*. New York: Brunner/Mazel.

Freeman, A. (1983). *Cognitive Therapy with Couples and Groups*. New York: Plenum.

Gil, E. (1987). *Children Who Molest: A Guide for Parents of Young Sex Offenders*. Walnut Creek, CA: Lauch Press.

Groth, A. N. (1977). The adolescent sexual offender and his prey. *International Journal of Offender Therapy and Comparative Criminology, 21,* 249-255.

Groth, A. N. (1982). The incest offender. In S. M. Sgroi (Ed.), *Handbook of Clinical Interventions in Child Sexual Abuse* (pp. 215-239). Lexington, MA: Lexington Books.

Groth, A. N., & Birnbaum, J. (1979). *Men Who Rape: The Psychology of the Offender*. New York: Plenum.

Groth, A. N., Hobson, W. F., Lucey, K. P., & St. Pierre, J. (1981). Juvenile sexual offenders: Guidelines for treatment. *International Journal of Offender Therapy and Comparative Criminology, 25,* 265-272.

Groth, A. N., Longo, R., & McFaden, J. (1982). Undetected recidivism among rapists and child molesters. *Crime and Delinquency, 128,* 450-458.

Groth, A. N., & Loredo, C. M. (1981). Juvenile sexual offenders: Guidelines for assessment. *International Journal of Offender Therapy and Comparative Criminology, 25,* 31-39.

Haley, J., & Madanes, C. (1989, May). *Family Therapy for Adolescent Sex Offenders*. Paper presented at Abuse in the Family: Sexual, Physical and Drug, sponsored by Knowledge Unlimited, Vancouver, B.C., Canada.

Haversack, G. (1982). Communication reported. In F. H. Knopp (Ed.), *Remedial Intervention in Adolescent Sex Offenses: Nine Program Descriptions* (p. 21). Orwell, VT: Safer Society Press.

Horner, R. H., Dunlap, G., & Koegel, R. L. (Eds.) (1988). *Generalization and Maintenance: Life Style Changes in Applied Settings.* Toronto, Ontario: H. Paul Brookes.

Jackson, J. F. (1984). *A Preliminary Survey of Adolescent Sex Offenses in New York: Remedies and Recommendations.* Orwell, VT: Safer Society Press.

James, B., & Nasjleti, M. (1983). *Treating Sexually Abused Children and Their Families.* Palo Alto, CA: Consulting Psychologists Press.

Johnson, T. C., & Berry, C. (1989). Children who molest: A treatment program. *Journal of Interpersonal Violence, 4,* 185-203.

Karoly, P., & Steffen, J. (Eds.). (1980). *Improving the Long-Term Effects of Psychotherapy: Models of Durable Outcome.* New York: Gardner.

Knopp, F. H. (1982). *Remedial Intervention in Adolescent Sex Offenses: Nine Program Descriptions.* Orwell, VT: Safer Society Press.

Knopp, F. H. (1985). *The Youthful Sex Offender: The Rationale and Goals of Early Intervention and Treatment.* Orwell, VT: Safer Society Press.

Knopp, F. H., & Lackey, L. B. (1987a). *Female Sexual Abusers: A Summary of Data from 44 Treatment Providers.* Orwell, VT: Safer Society Press.

Knopp, F. H., & Lackey, L. B. (1987b). *Sexual Offenders Identified as Intellectually Disabled: A Summary of Data from 40 Treatment Providers.* Orwell, VT: Safer Society Press.

Knopp, F. H., & Stevenson, W. F. (1988). *Nationwide Survey of Juvenile and Adult Sex Offender Treatment Programs and Models.* Orwell, VT: Safer Society Press.

Lafond, M. (1982). Sex offender therapy program - Echo Glen. In F. H. Knopp (Ed.), *Remedial Intervention in Adolescent Sex Offenses: Nine Program Descriptions* (pp. 91-102). Orwell, VT: Safer Society Press.

Lanyon, R. I. (1986). Theory and treatment in child molestation. *Journal of Consulting and Clinical Psychology, 54,* 176-182.

Lewis, D. O., Shanok, S., & Pincus, J. (1981). Juvenile male sexual assaulters: Psychiatric, neurological, psychoeducational and abuse factors. In D. O. Lewis (Ed.), *Vulnerability to*

Delinquency (pp. 89-105). Jamaica, NY: Spectrum Publications.

Longo, R. E., & Groth, A. N. (1983). Juvenile sexual offenses in the histories of adult rapists and child molesters. *International Journal of Offender Therapy and Comparative Criminology, 27,* 150-155.

Maloney, M. P. (1985). *A Clinician's Guide to Forensic Psychological Assessments.* New York: Free Press.

Margolin, L. (1983). A treatment model for the adolescent sex offender. *Journal of Offender Counselling, Services and Rehabilitation, 8,* 1-12.

Margolin, L. (1984). Group therapy as a means of learning about the sexually assaultive adolescent. *International Journal of Offender Therapy and Comparative Criminology, April,* 65-72.

Mathews, F. (1987). *Adolescent Sex Offenders: A Need Study.* Toronto, Ontario, Canada: Central Toronto Youth Services.

Mathews, F. (1989). *Towards a National Strategy for Treatment of Child Abuse Victims, Their Families and Offenders. Reaching for Solutions.* Ottawa, Ontario, Canada: Health & Welfare Canada.

Mathews, F., & Stermac, L. (1988). *Adolescent Sex Offenders: A Tracking Study.* Toronto, Ontario, Canada: Central Toronto Youth Services.

Mathews, R., Mathews, J. K., & Speltz, K. (1989). *Female Sexual Offenders.* Orwell, VT: Safer Society Press.

Meichenbaum, D., & Turk, D. (1987). *Facilitating Treatment Adherence: A Practitioner's Guide.* New York: Plenum.

Monahan, J. (Ed.). (1980). *Who is the Client? The Ethics of Psychological Intervention in the Criminal Justice System.* Washington, DC: American Psychological Association.

Naar, R. (1982). *A Premier of Group Psychotherapy.* New York: Sciences Press.

National Task Force on Juvenile Sexual Offending (Preliminary Report). (1988). *Juvenile Family Court Journal, 39,* 1-67.

O'Brien, M. J. (1989). *Characteristics of Male Adolescent Sibling Incest Offenders: Preliminary Findings.* Orwell, VT: Safer Society Press.

O'Brien, M. J., & Bera, W. H. (1986). Adolescent sexual offenders: A descriptive typology. *Preventing Sexual Abuse, 1,* 1-4.

Orchard, J., & Perry, G. P. (1989). *Services to Adolescent Sex Offenders: Continuum of Services.* Unpublished manuscript.

Paquin, M. J., & Perry, G. P. (1990). Maintaining successful intervention in social, vocational and community rehabilitation. *The Canadian Journal of Community Mental Health, 9,* 39-49.

Perry, G. P., & Orchard, J. M. (1989). Assessment and treatment of adolescent sex offenders. In P. A. Keller & S. R. Heyman (Eds.), *Innovations in Clinical Practice: A Source Book* (Vol. 8, pp. 187-211). Sarasota, FL: Professional Resource Exchange.

Perry, G. P., & Paquin, M. J. (1987). Practical strategies for maintaining and generalizing improvements from psychotherapy. In P. A. Keller & S. R. Heyman (Eds.), *Innovations in Clinical Practice: A Source Book* (Vol. 6, pp. 151-164). Sarasota, FL: Professional Resource Exchange.

Pithers, W. D., Kashima, K. M., Cumming, G. F., & Beal, L. S. (1988). Relapse prevention: A method of enhancing maintenance of change in sex offenders. In A. C. Salter, *Treating Child Sex Offenders and Victims: A Practical Guide* (pp. 131-170). Newbury Park, CA: Sage.

Quay, H. C. (1987). *Handbook of Juvenile Delinquency.* New York: Wiley-Interscience Publications.

Reid, C., Orchard, J., & Sandre, L. (1991). *Technique Devised for Offender Treatment Group.* Unpublished manuscript, Windsor, Ontario.

Richardson, J., Loss, P., & Ross, J. E. (1988). *Psychoeducational Curriculum for the Adolescent Sex Offender.* (Order by contacting Ross, Loss & Associates, P.O. Box 666, Mystic, CT 06355-0666.)

Rogers, R. G. (1988). *An Overview of Issues and Concerns Related to the Sexual Abuse of Children in Canada.* Ottawa, Ontario, Canada: Health & Welfare Canada.

Rosenbaum, M. (1983). *Handbook of Short-Term Therapy Groups.* New York: McGraw-Hill.

Ross, J. (1988). Group treatment approaches. In *Proceedings of the Training Intensive for the Treatment of Adolescent Sex Offenders Workshop May/88, Toronto, Ontario* (pp. 43-64). Ottawa, Ontario, Canada: Child Welfare Association.

Ross, J. (1989, April). *Group Treatment Approaches.* Paper presented at Advanced Training for Treatment of Adolescent Sex Offenders. Sponsored by Canadian Child Welfare Association, Toronto, Ontario.

Ross, J. E., Loss, P., & Associates. (1988). *Risk Assessment/Interviewing Protocol for Adolescent Sex Offenders.*

(Order by contacting Ross, Loss & Associates, P.O. Box 666, Mystic, CT 06355-0666.)

Ryan, C. (1986). Annotated bibliography. Adolescent perpetrators of sexual molestation of children. *Child Abuse & Neglect, 10,* 125-131.

Salter, A. C. (1988). *Treating Child Sex Offenders and Victims: A Practical Guide.* Newbury Park, CA: Sage.

Simon, S. B., Howe, L. W., & Kirschenbaum, H. (1978). *Values Clarification: A Handbook of Practical Strategies for Teachers and Students.* New York: Dodd, Mead & Co.

Smets, A. C., & Cebula, C. (1987). A group treatment program for adolescent sex offenders: Five steps towards resolution. *Child Abuse and Neglect, 11,* 247-254.

Smith, W. R. (1985). *Juvenile Sex Offenders and the Prediction of Risk.* Paper presented at Adolescent Perpetrator Meetings arranged by Centre, Keystone, Colorado.

Smith, W. R., & Monastersky, C. (1986). Assessing juvenile sex offenders' risk for re-offending. *Criminal Justice and Behavior, 13,* 115-140.

Stermac, L., & Mathews, F. (1987). *Adolescent Sex Offenders: Towards a Profile.* Toronto, Ontario, Canada. Central Toronto Youth Services.

Stokes, T. F., & Baer, D. M. (1977). An implicit technology of generalization. *Journal of Applied Behavior Analysis, 10,* 349-367

Stout, G. E. (1987). Integrated forensic evaluation form for adolescents. In P. A. Keller & S. R. Heyman (Eds.), *Innovations in Clinical Practice: A Source Book* (Vol. 6, pp. 289-294). Sarasota, FL: Professional Resource Exchange.

Toufexis, A. (1989, June). Teenagers and sex crimes: A New Jersey assault dramatizes the rise in offenses by youths. *Time,* p. 57.

Van Ness, S. R. (1984). Rape as instrumental violence: A study of youth offenders. *Journal of Offender Counselling Services and Rehabilitation, 9,* 161-170.

Wenet, G. A., & Clark, T. R. (1983). *Decision Criterion: Juvenile Sexual Offender Program.* Seattle, WA: University of Washington.

Westphal, K. L., & Kohn, S. H. (1984). The expert witness: Techniques and skills. In S. J. Weaver (Ed.), *Testing Children: A Reference Guide for Effective Clinical and Psychoeducational Assessments* (pp. 220-232). Kansas City, MO: Wesport Publishers.

INDEX

A

Abel, G. G., 4, 7, 8, 10
Abuse, 48-49
    emotional, 13, 41-42
    physical, 13, 25, 37, 41-42, 49, 50, 51, 54, 83
    sexual, 9-10, 13, 18, 22, 25, 37, 41-42, 49, 50, 51, 54, 77, 83
Academic functioning, 37
Accountability
    of offenders, 73, 76, 82
    of treatment programs, 107
Aggression, 5, 8, 40, 50, 52
Alcohol, 15
Alcoholics, 5
Alligator River Exercise, 23-24, 76
Anchor, K. N., 26
Anger, 5, 10, 11, 13, 18, 83
Anger management, 45, 49, 65, 71, 79, 86, 90
Apologies to victims, 78, 83, 96, 97
Araji, S., 17
Assertiveness, 13, 64, 65, 75, 79, 86, 102
Assessment, 6, 13, 26, 31-61, 68
    case example, 55-61
    format of, 34-61
    goals of, 31
    of group candidates, 86-87

Assessment *(Continued)*
  initial interview with offender, 36-45, 54, 111-114
  legal aspects of, 31, 32, 34
  mistakes, 43-45
  parent interviews, 47-50, 54, 115-118
  psychological testing, 36, 45-47
  report, 51, 54-61
  unique aspects of, 32
Audiovisual media, 68

B

Babysitting, 7, 16, 25, 48
Baer, D. M., 99
Bengis, S. M., 4, 6, 10, 11, 22, 50, 51, 119
Bera, W. H., 6, 9, 17, 18, 35, 37
Berry, C., 1, 4
Birnbaum, J., 1
Blame, externalization of, 81, 83
Blaming victims, 15, 41
Blau, T. H., 26
Booster sessions, 105
Breer, W., 6, 10, 11, 64, 94, 95
Burchard, J. D., 26
Burchard, S. N., 26
Burnout, 29, 89
Byrne, K., 26

C

Case management, 87-89
Case study sample, 90-92
Cebula, C., 64
Clark, T. R., 50
Clarkin, J., 53
Classification of offenders, 17-19
Closed-custody placement, 6, 33, 34, 123-124
Co-leaders' issues, 22
Cognitive functioning, 12-13, 37
Coleman, E., 6, 11
Community-based treatment, 6, 33, 67-97
Community placement, 33
Confidentiality, 31, 32, 34, 37, 72

Continuum of service model, 19, 33, 51
Contracts, 101, 103
Control issues, 5, 8, 37, 40, 43, 49, 68, 82
Corder, B. F., 26
Cormier, L. S., 25
Cormier, W. H., 25
Court experience, 26
Creeden, K., 67
Cunninggim, P., 6

D

Dating, 13, 77, 79, 86, 102
Davis, G. E., 5, 9, 10, 41, 49
Defense mechanisms, 11, 13, 38
    denial, 11, 12-13, 14-15, 32, 35, 37, 38, 41, 45, 50, 64, 65, 74,
        82, 85, 95
    minimization, 13, 32, 35, 38, 41, 65, 74, 78, 81, 82, 95
    projection, 11, 12, 82
    rationalization, 11, 12, 18, 37, 40, 41, 65, 74, 78, 81, 82
Delinquency, 16, 26, 37, 42, 45, 50
Denial
    by offender, 11, 12-13, 32, 35, 37, 38, 41, 45, 50, 64, 65, 74, 82,
        85, 95
    by parents, 13, 14, 50, 94
    patterns of, 14-15
Depression, 5, 45
Discipline, 49
Disturbed impulsive, 18, 68
Drawbacks of working with offenders, 29-30
Dreiblatt, I. S., 50, 51, 119

E

Education
    of offender, 37, 38, 64, 65, 75, 76, 77, 78, 85-86, 94-95, 100-
        101
    of parents, 47-48, 94-95
Egan, G., 25
Empathy, 12, 14, 24, 25, 39, 40, 65, 71, 81, 82-83, 88
Enfield, R., 26
Environmental factors, 15
Evaluation, 89-90, 93

Evans, D. R., 25
Exercises
    feeling, 78
    perception of offenders, 27-28
    values clarification, 23-24
Exhibitionism, 4, 5 (*See also* Exposing)
Experimentation, 1, 8, 17
Exposing, 11, 18 (*See also* Exhibitionism)

F

Family
    denial, 13, 14, 50
    involvement, 13, 16, 52, 93-97, 101, 104
    issues, 10, 11, 18, 37, 42, 47-50, 54, 79
    placement, 33, 125
Family Assessment Measure, 45-47
Family therapy, 64, 67, 68, 71, 88, 93-97, 102
Fantasies, 11, 12, 14, 15, 16, 37, 40, 42, 54, 76, 77, 82, 84, 101
Fathers, 11
Feeling identification, 78, 83, 86
Fersch, Jr., E. A., 34
Finckenauer, J. O., 26
Finkelhor, D., 17
First offense, 9
Follow-up treatment, 33, 99-100
Fondling, 5
Forensic assessments, 26, 32
Foster home placement, 33, 124-125
Four-week cycle of group therapy, 74-75
Frances, A., 53
Freeman, A., 26

G

Generalization techniques, 99, 100, 102, 103
Gil, E., 95, 101
GMT techniques, 99-100, 102, 103
Go-around, 72, 73-74
Gratification, 5
Groth, A. N., 1, 3, 4, 7, 17, 37, 50

Group-influenced offender, 18, 68
Group leaders
    tasks of, 86-88
    time allocation of, 87-88
Group therapy, 67-86
    acceptance criteria for, 68-71
    co-leaders of, 68
    go-around, 72, 73-74
    intake, 69
    involvement of referral source, 70
    language criteria, 68-69, 72
    number of participants, 69
    objectives of, 71, 81
    planned termination from, 69, 75
    rationale for, 67
    referral sources to, 69
    rules of, 72-73
    schedule of meetings, 69
    strategies used, 71
    structure of, 67-86
    techniques in, 76-86
Group therapy model, 26
Guilt, 13, 14, 18

H

Haley, J., 96, 97
High-risk offenders, qualities of, 53, 119-122
Homework
    for offenders, 68, 72, 76, 79, 82, 85, 90, 103
    for parents, 95
Howe, L. W., 24

I

Individual therapy, 64, 67, 68, 88, 93
Information, sources of, in assessment, 35-36
Intervention
    midtherapy, 102-104
    posttherapy, 100, 104-105
    pretherapy, 100-102
    stages of, 99-105

J

Jackson, J. F., 10, 11, 119
Jesness Behavior Checklist, 45
Jesness Inventory, 45
Johnson, T. C., 1, 4
Journal, 76, 87, 101, 102, 103-104

K

Kirschenbaum, H., 24
Knopp, F. H., 4, 11
Kohn, S. H., 26

L

Lackey, L. B., 1
Lafond, M., 107
Language criteria, 68-69
Lanyon, R. I., 4
Leitenberg, H., 5, 9, 10, 41, 49
Lewis, D. O., 10
Limits, 25, 64
Listening skills
    offender, 83
    therapist, 25
Literature, 3, 107-108
Longo, R. E., 4
Loredo, C. M., 3, 37
Loss, P., 1, 5, 6, 17, 36, 37
Low-risk offenders, qualities of, 119-122

M

Madanes, C., 96, 97
Maintenance techniques, 99, 100, 102, 103
Maloney, M. P., 26
Masturbation, 4, 11, 21, 42, 77, 84
Mathews, F., 7

McFaden, J., 4
Midtherapy intervention, 102-104
Minimization
    offender, 3-4, 13, 14, 32, 35, 38, 41, 65, 74, 78, 81, 82, 95
    parents, 50
Monahan, J., 26
Mothers, characteristics of, 11
Motivation for treatment, 52, 54
Motivation to offend, 5, 8, 11, 18
Myths, 3, 6-10, 48, 63-64, 82

N

Naar, R., 26
Naïve experimenter, 17, 68, 95
National Clearinghouse on Family Violence, 78
National Task Force on Juvenile Sexual Offending, 21-22, 25, 29,
    76
No-treatment decisions, 53

O

O'Brien, M. J., 17, 18
Obscene telephone calls, 5
Offense patterns, 39, 41, 63, 65, 74, 75, 80, 83, 84
Open-custody placement, 33, 34, 124
Orchard, J. M., 1, 4, 6, 19, 33, 50, 51, 53, 83, 119

P

Paquin, M. J., 99, 102
Parents
    interviews, 36, 47-50, 54, 115-118
    marital relationship, 49-50, 51, 54
    role in treatment, 13, 16, 48, 52, 93-97, 101, 104
Patterns of offense, 39, 41, 63, 65, 74, 75, 80, 83, 84
Peeping, 11, 18 (*See also* Voyeurism)
Peer age assault, 9
Peer relationships, 11, 13, 16, 18, 36, 37, 42, 50, 54
Perry, G. P., 1, 4, 6, 19, 33, 50, 51, 53, 99, 100, 102, 119
Perry, S., 53
PHASE (Program for Healthy Adolescent Sexual Expression), 35
Pincus, J., 10

Pithers, W. D., 78, 82, 84, 103
Placement options, 6, 32-33, 42, 47, 53-54, 123-125
Planning of offenses, 5, 8, 14, 15
Pornography, 42, 77
Posttherapy intervention, 100, 104-105
Pretherapy intervention, 100-102
Program for Healthy Adolescent Sexual Expression (PHASE), 35
Projection, 11, 12, 82
Pseudo-socialized child exploiter, 18, 68
Psychiatric inpatient placement, 33
Psychological testing, 36, 45-47, 87
Psychotherapy, individual, 64, 67, 68, 88, 93, 102

Q

Quay, H. C., 26

R

Rape myths, 21
Rapport
    with offender, 37, 38-39
    with parents, 47
Rationalization, 11, 12, 18, 37, 40, 41, 65, 74, 78, 81, 82
Raven's Standard Progressive Matrices, 46
Reaching-out exercises, 79
Recidivism, 90, 108
Reeducation, 85-86
Reenactment of offenses, 78
Referral sources, 69, 70
Reid, C., 83
Relapse prevention, 73, 75, 78, 79, 80-81, 82, 84, 103, 105
Reoffending patterns, 38
Research, 4, 10, 107-108
Residential treatment, 6
Responsibility, acceptance of, 81-82, 90
Rewards of working with offenders, 28
Richardson, J., 5, 94, 100, 101
Risk Checklist, 51, 52, 86, 119-122
Risk Factor Constellation, 51, 52, 123-125
Risk of re-offending, 6, 8, 14-15, 32, 34, 37, 38, 50-52, 54, 80, 86,
        103, 119-122, 123-125
Rogers, R. G., 1

Role playing, 78, 79, 86
Rosenbaum, M., 26
Ross, J. E., 1, 5, 6, 17, 36, 37, 42, 83, 101

S

Salter, A. C., 13, 14, 76
Sandre, L., 83
Sanford, L., 67
Secretary, group, 76
Selection of offenders, 100
Sex Knowledge History, 46
Sex offender-specific treatment, definition of, 6
Sex offenders
    adult, 7
    age of, 1
    characteristics of, 1, 3, 7
    classification of, 17-19
    definition of, 4-5
    female, 1, 7
    gender of, 1
    initial offenses, 4
    myths, 3, 6-10, 48
    problem areas of, 11
    typology of, 1-2, 3
    vulnerability to re-offend, 7-8
Sex-role attitudes, 12, 65, 76, 82, 85
Sexual aggressive, 18, 68
Sexual assault, motivation for, 5, 8, 11, 18
Sexual attitudes
    of offenders, 10, 42, 76, 77, 78, 85
    of therapists, 21-24, 29-30
Sexual autobiography, 76, 77
Sexual compulsive, 18, 68
Sexual identity, 11, 85, 86
Sexual offenses, planning of, 5, 8, 14, 15
Shanok, S., 10
Siblings, 15, 16, 82
Significant others, 13
Simon, S. B., 24
Skill-training programs, 6, 68, 71, 79, 102
Smets, A. C., 64
Smith, W. R., 53

Social relationships of offenders, 12, 17, 18, 37, 49, 50, 79
Social skills, 10, 11, 13, 71, 86, 90, 102
Soliciting, 11
Stereotypes, 6-10, 12, 65, 76, 82, 85
Stokes, T. F., 99
Stout, G. E., 26
Stress-coping skills, 13, 64, 86
Substance abuse, 13, 18, 37, 42, 48, 49, 50, 51
Suicidal ideation, 42
Suppression, 85
Survival strategy, 83-85

T

Termination, 69, 75, 79, 105
Testing, 36, 45-47, 87
Therapist interactions, 68
Therapist issues, 21-30
    clinical skills, 24-25
    group leader qualifications, 75
    personal issues, 22-24
    positive and negative aspects, 28-30
    professional qualities, 26, 27-28
    response to discussion of offenses, 21-22
    sexual attitudes and beliefs, 21-24
    training of, 21-22, 27, 88-89
Therapy, family, 64, 67, 68, 71, 88, 93-97, 102
Therapy, foci for, 10-16
"To a Safer Place," 78
Toufexis, A., 4
Training of therapists, 21-22, 27, 88-90
Transfer techniques, 99, 100, 102, 103
Treatment
    alternatives, 32-33, 63-64
    approaches, 71
    community-based, 67-97
    generic, 6
    goals of, 64-65
    issues, 64-65
    length of, 76, 104-105
    plan, 31
    progress criteria, 90
    stages of, 64

U

Underreporting, 3, 6
Undersocialized child exploiter, 17-18, 68

V

Values clarification, 23-24, 68, 76, 85
Vampire syndrome, 9
Van Ness, S. R., 10
Victims, 24, 28, 31, 38, 39, 48, 49
    access to, 15-16
    age of, 7, 11, 50
    apologies to, 78, 83, 96, 97
    attitudes toward, 41
    blaming, 15, 41
    demeaning terms for, 41
    fantasies about, 40
    feelings of, 3
    films of, 76, 78, 82
    interviewing, 35
    known versus not known, 7
    number of, 4, 8, 50
    perceptions of, 24, 50
    reparation toward, 96, 97
    use of first names of, 72, 74, 83
Videotapes, 78, 79
Voyeurism, 4, 5 (*See also* Peeping)

W

Wechsler Adult Intelligence Scale - Revised, 46-47
Wechsler Intelligence Scale for Children, 46
Wenet, G. A., 50
Westphal, K. L., 26
Witness, expert, 26
Women as authority, 68
Written assignments, 78

If You Found This Book Useful . . .

You might want to know more about our other titles.

If you would like to receive our latest catalog, please return this form:

Name: _____
(Please Print)

Address: _____

Address: _____

City/State/Zip: _____
This is ☐ home ☐ office

Telephone: (_____) _____

I am a:

☐ Psychologist   ☐ Mental Health Counselor
☐ Psychiatrist   ☐ Marriage and Family Therapist
☐ School Psychologist   ☐ Not in Mental Health Field
☐ Clinical Social Worker   ☐ Other: _____

◆   ◆   ◆

Professional Resource Press
P.O. Box 15560
Sarasota, FL 34277-1560

Telephone: 800-443-3364
FAX: 941-343-9201
E-mail: mail@prpress.com
Website: http://www.prpress.com

ATA/07/01

Add A Colleague To Our Mailing List . . .

If you would like us to send our latest catalog to one of your colleagues, please return this form:

Name: _____
(Please Print)

Address: _____

Address: _____

City/State/Zip: _____
This is ☐ home ☐ office

Telephone: (_____)_____

This person is a:

☐ Psychologist   ☐ Mental Health Counselor
☐ Psychiatrist   ☐ Marriage and Family Therapist
☐ School Psychologist   ☐ Not in Mental Health Field
☐ Clinical Social Worker   ☐ Other: _____

Name of person completing this form: _____

◆   ◆   ◆

Professional Resource Press
P.O. Box 15560
Sarasota, FL 34277-1560

Telephone: 800-443-3364
FAX: 941-343-9201
E-mail: mail@prpress.com
Website: http://www.prpress.com

ATA/07/01